Direct Marketing Checklists

John Stockwell

Henry Shaw

NTC Business Books
a division of *NTC Publishing Group* • Lincolnwood, Illinois USA

Library of Congress Cataloging-in-Publication Data

Stockwell, John.
        Direct marketing checklists/John Stockwell, Henry Shaw.
            p.   cm.
        ISBN 0-8442-3224-6
            1. Direct marketing—Planning.   I. Shaw, Henry (Henry M.)
II. Title.
HF5415.126.S755   1993
658.8'4—dc20   93-6694
                                                                  CIP

Published by NTC Business Books, a division of NTC Publishing Group
4255 West Touhy Avenue
Lincolnwood (Chicago), Illinois 60646-1975, U.S.A.
©1994 by NTC Publishing Group. All rights reserved.
No part of this book may be reproduced, stored in a retrieval system,
or transmitted in any form or by any means,
electronic, mechanical, photocopying, recording or otherwise,
without the prior permission of NTC Publishing Group.
Manufactured in the United States of America.

3 4 5 6 7 8 9 ML 9 8 7 6 5 4 3 2 1

Contents

Introduction

Direct response marketing—whether by mail, space advertising in newspapers or magazines, television, or telemarketing—presents a whole new series of marketing challenges. You may be a newcomer to this field or a long-time pro, but the questions you must answer will determine your company's growth and profits, your career advancement, and ultimately your personal and corporate future.

1. How do I get into a direct response operation with minimum risk of making terrible mistakes and losing money?

2. How can I find out whether I can market my product using direct response techniques?

3. How can I estimate the size of my market and its profit potential?

4. How do I handle all the nitty-gritty details of creating advertisements, choosing media and mailing lists, getting the best results from a fixed budget, and analyzing results for future growth decision?

You will face hundreds of questions such as these, but virtually none of them will be unique to you. Others have faced similar questions in the past and have discovered tested techniques that can be applied to almost every situation.

The beauty of direct marketing is that its results are by nature *measurable*. This means that you can learn directly from the programs and the tests that others have conducted. There is no need to reinvent the wheel every time you make a direct marketing decision. In this book, we have taken the tried and tested principles of direct marketing and condensed them into a comprehensive series of checklists, worksheets, tables, and forms. The checklists will guide you step-by-step through every direct marketing decision you make.

These outlines, and the accompanying commentaries, are useful in several ways: first, they insure against forgetting some essential detail—something even the most experienced marketing manager will do on occasion. Secondly, they organize your thinking, planning, and *doing* to such an extent that you can be sure you are doing the best possible job every time.

The forms and charts presented in the book can be used exactly as is, or you can revise, change, expand, improve, or customize them to your own particular needs.

Direct Marketing Checklists shows you how to get the most sales from every marketing dollar spent in this medium. Whether you are considering direct response for the first time, or are a long-time veteran in the field, this manual will help you develop a model direct marketing plan and execute it efficiently to increase sales, reduce expenses, minimize errors and omissions, and exploit your market to the fullest.

John Stockwell
Henry Shaw

PART I
Planning for Direct Marketing Campaigns

- **3 Checklists to Define Direct Marketing Goals**
- **10 Checklists for Product Planning**
- **7 Checklists for Conducting Marketing Research**
- **4 Checklists for Forecasting Market Potential**
- **5 Checklists for Forecasting Sales**

3 Checklists to Define Direct Marketing Goals

Often, top management will decide that the company's products can be sold by direct response and will then lay the responsibility for such sales on an existing department. To ensure success, there should be agreement *from the beginning* about what is important, even before discussing profits, expenses, and other quantitative details.

In some companies, direct response is the only source of sales and income, while in others, direct response may be used as an adjunct for some other purpose—to help meet corporate goals, for example. The purpose may be, among others:

- To support a dealer or sales network

- To reach markets not served by existing sales outlets

- To generate inquiries for the sales force

- To reach a niche market

- To test new products

- To increase awareness of the company among qualified prospects

The most important step is to get agreement from all concerned—from top management to the ranks that will do the work— about precisely what is desired of the operation. By committing your company's direct response goals to paper, you will always have a basic philosophy to guide you. It will help you see how your direct marketing goals fit in with overall corporate goals. It will also help you in the future when you set budgets, decide on staffing, analyze results, or decide to change the goals.

GOAL SETTING **Checklist 1,** Direct Response Goals Worksheet, will help you determine goals *and* decide their importance. Take your time to fill in this checklist. It is not a job to be hurried; all your future decisions will depend on what you discover here. Consider this worksheet as a jumping-off point for a company strategic marketing planning meeting. Copy it onto a chalkboard or easel pad and fill it with input from all concerned. As the discussion progresses and agreement emerges, you should arrive at corporate goals that will serve as the starting point for all future plans.

Remember, you are seeking consensus about your goals and approval from management. This can be critical, because if you are convinced that your goal is, say, a certain percentage response rate on your mailings, but management is less concerned about response rate and is more interested in gaining awareness of the product, you could win the battle and lose the war. That is, you could accomplish *your* goals but not management's. This disparity of goals can be avoided by having agreement up front about your direct response goals and priorities.

Once you have completed Checklist 1, you will have determined the relative importance to you and your company of each goal. The next step is to rank each of your goals in order of priority.

Checklist 2, Setting and Prioritizing Goals, will help you do three things:

- Rank goals in order of importance

- Clearly define each goal

- Set dates by which each goal should be accomplished

The following paragraphs provide guidelines for completing Checklist 2.

Goal 1 The first goal should be the most important thing you want to accomplish. It should be clearly defined and understood by everyone involved. It might be too early to quantify your primary goal—how can you put down a sales number if you haven't even determined the size of your market? However, you should strive to come up with an unambiguous statement that everyone understands. Sample statements might be as follows:

- To generate direct response profits, as a percentage of sales, equal to the average company profit or better.

- To add incremental income that exceeds direct response expenses and overhead, thereby adding to corporate profitability.

- To create profitable niche market areas beyond the customers now served, thereby expanding our business.

Put as simply as possible, the primary goal should address the big problems faced by your company—the kind of things that keep you or the boss awake at night.

Goal 2 The second goal should be important, but not up to the measure of the first. Establishing the single most important goal as number one is important, but in the number two spot you might list two or more goals that have equal validity. No problem! Put them all down. Sample statements of secondary goals might be as follows:

- To help our field force increase sales through the support of direct response campaigns.

- To test market new products more economically than using our present methods.

- To increase the productivity of existing resources by creating and running a direct response operation without adding to staff.

These are not the great concerns addressed in the first goal; they are the kinds of problems and challenges that appeal to middle management, who are generally concerned about the effective utilization of existing resources to generate incremental business. Every conscientious manager wants to see the company make more money and avoid waste. This is what ultimately makes a job rewarding.

Goal 3   The third goal should be the kind of result that would be nice to achieve as a by-product of reaching the first two goals. It is not a goal that is worth the same degree of attention, expense, and risk as number one, but it would benefit the company if it were achieved. Again, you will probably find more than one goal here. Sample statements might be as follows:

- To build into our response (sales) mechanisms more demographic information about our customers so that we can segment our lists more efficiently and increase sales.

- To build a mailing list that we can rent for additional income.

- To maintain a presence in the marketplace so we don't lose out to our competitors.

THE IMPORTANCE OF CONTINUAL GOAL SETTING   Do not skimp on the goal-setting phase of planning. Even if your company has run a direct response operation for years, reviewing goals and gaining organizational consensus for them is good strategy for two reasons:

- After some years, a company may evolve conflicting goals that will be made more apparent after reviewing them. For example, a company may want its direct response manager to bring in sales at a certain level of profit. At the same time, management may insist that certain mailings be made as part of a publicity effort or for market research. You can't have it both ways and still make a profit.

- You will simplify your job and eliminate rationalizing your activities to your boss or higher management if the goals are clear and accepted by everyone. Everything you do or decide not to do can be measured against the agreed-on yardstick.

This goal orientation does not require blind adherence to the past. Goals should be flexible and constantly re-examined in the light of current experience. Moreover, your goal should have checkpoints along the way so that course corrections can be made if needed. For example: "By June 1, a new order form will be created that will give us more demographic information about our customers." By using dates to verify activity or increased sales as checkpoints, broadly stated goals can be made measurable. Goals that are vaguely stated cannot be measured objectively.

Checklist 3, Quantifying Marketing Objectives, provides a format for you to translate such vague or general goals into specific objectives linked to percentage or dollar values and a commitment to a specific date for achievement. Each objective of this type should have the approval of management and the full understanding and commitment of the entire organization. For example, the goal "to build a mailing list that we can rent for additional income" would translate into an objective in Checklist 3 as follows:

To create a mailing list of 15,000 buyers during the next 12 months, to generate $10,000 in additional income by June 1.

10 Checklists for Product Planning

Before you embark on a direct response program, you need to know **what** the benefits of your product are, **who** will purchase the product (the target market), **where** to reach prospective customers, **how many** there are, and **how much** they are willing to pay. The next section will help you make a very important planning decision—you'll decide whether or not your product is suited to direct response selling.

IS DIRECT RESPONSE RIGHT FOR YOUR PRODUCT?

It has been said over and over that virtually any product can be sold via direct response. Think of a mundane product available at any local market—say, a bag of onions. Your first response might be that such a product is bound to fail as a direct response product because it is so easily and economically available locally. Yet a specialized farm sells "gourmet" onions by mail quite successfully, using space advertising in upscale magazines. This example demonstrates the truth of the statement that almost anything can be sold through direct response. However, certain products are generally easier to sell and easier to ship. Before you continue with your campaign, pull out **Checklist 4,** Verifying Product Suitability for Direct Response Sales.

The questions in Checklist 4 deal with issues that may not be immediately apparent as potential problems, but it will help you weed out unsuitable products even before you get into such questions as costs, profit margins, prospects or buyers lists, production, and the like.

Once you have decided that your product *is* suited to direct response selling, you are ready to begin preliminary product planning. There are three questions critical to proper planning. They are as follows:

- Have all product benefits been clarified?

- Has the target market been identified?

- Can the target market be segmented?

Use the next three checklists to answer these questions.

DEFINING PRODUCT BENEFITS

Why should people buy your product? Determining the *consumer benefits* of your product is key to conducting a successful campaign. Use **Checklist 5,** Determining Product Attributes and Benefits, to describe all the benefits your customers will gain from using your product. Remember, product features—the special attributes that your product possesses—are not benefits. They only become benefits when you can translate them into characteristics that improve your customers' performance. For example, a salon-quality shampoo may have the product attribute of superior rinseability. This attribute must be translated into a benefit that is of importance to the user—clean, shiny, healthy hair. Don't expect prospective customers to interpret what product attributes mean to them. In direct response, the customer benefits must be clear and attention-getting from the start.

IDENTIFYING THE TARGET MARKET

Identifying the target market is not always an easy process. First you must recognize the target market's attributes so that you can build a profile of your intended customers. **Checklist 6,** Establishing Target Market Profiles, will walk you through the basics of building a picture of your target market. It is broken into three sections:

I. **Demographics.** The vital statistics of age, gender, income, and education of your target market allow you to plan all aspects of your direct response campaign. Families with young children vary dramatically in their purchasing habits from older couples whose children have all left the family home. You must clearly identify which groups are most likely to be interested in your product or service.

II. **Psychographics.** Psychographics refers to life-style, and your target market will probably have a unique life-style. You may be interested to know your potential customers' travel habits or their interest in photography or computers.

III. **Location.** Another aspect of your target market that may be valuable to know is where they live. If your strategy includes supporting retail sales, you will want to know where the outlets are located. If climate affects sales, you will need to know where to mail. The more you know about your customers, the more effective your direct mail can be.

IDENTIFYING TARGET MARKET SEGMENTS

Once you have identified your target market using Checklist 6, you should attempt to divide that market into segments. These segments will be people with similar demographics, psychographics, or geographics or some combination of the three. If you can segment them, you may find that you can tailor your sales message to each segment for a greater response. It is important to remember that too small a segment size may be cost prohibitive. For example, if it costs $1,000 to alter your cover letter for one segment, and your most optimistic estimate is that you will gain an incremental sale of $900 to that segment, that strategy should probably be abandoned.

After you segment your target market, if some of the segments are too small to warrant the extra expense and effort of tailoring your campaign to them, see whether you can combine some of them so that the tailoring process pays off. Now use **Checklist 7,** Segmenting Markets, to list and quantify each segment.

QUALIFYING MARKET SEGMENTS

Next, try this brief reality check to make sure that your segmentation efforts can be translated into useful information. Once you have divided your target market into discrete segments, make sure you have the resources available to enable you to reach them. Answer these questions:

- Are lists or other resources available to reach the target market?

- Is the target market large enough to warrant your time and expense?

- Is the target market willing to pay the price you require to purchase the product?

To answer these questions, you'll need first to estimate the base cost of implementing your direct marketing program to its core target market. You'll then have to estimate the incremental costs to be incurred if you decide, in addition, to target specific segments of that market. The costs may include preparation and printing of the direct response package, as well as the costs of acquiring mailing lists, sorting, and postage for each segment. Look at **Checklist 8,** Qualifying Target Segments. In Column B, estimate the additional cost likely to be incurred by targeting each additional segment. In Column C, estimate the maximum increase in sales targeting that segment will result in. If Column C does not significantly exceed column B, it may be best to abandon that segment or combine it with another segment.

Checklist 9, Quantifying Marketing Objectives by Target Market Segment, provides another method of checking your sales goals against the market segments you have decided to target. You will give each market segment a sales objective, in units, and multiply the units sold by unit price to derive the anticipated revenue from each market. You will then be able to judge which segments of the market are most important for the company's total revenue and adjust your advertising and marketing plans accordingly.

SELECTING NEW PRODUCTS

Before you create a direct marketing campaign for any product, be sure that you can answer these two questions.

- Is this a product that will be accepted immediately by your target market?

- Is this a new product or technology that will require extensive explanation or demonstration?

If you answer *yes* to the second question, this means you will need to educate your potential customer to the product, its attributes and benefits, before they will buy. **Checklist 10,** Calculating the Cost of Educating Customers, will help you factor in the cost—in both time and dollar terms—of educating customers.

PRICING PRODUCTS

The price of any product must be set high enough to cover costs and make a profit but low enough so that customers are willing to purchase the product. The checklist below compares the gross profit of different price strategies. Generally, as you lower the price, the number of units you will sell will increase—to a point. Use **Checklist 11,** Pricing Strategy, to calculate the *gross profit* expected from each product price. (See Appendix A for a detailed explanation of how to calculate gross profit.)

In addition to calculating gross profit, you must take into consideration the prices charged by your competitors for the same or similar items. If customers perceive your product as having a higher value than those of your competitors, you might be able to charge a higher price. **Checklist 12,** Competitive Price Comparison, will help you settle on the right price.

PRODUCT LIFE CYCLE

Every product has its own distinct life cycle. Your product's life-cycle stage should affect how it is marketed. The matrix below shows how to tell what stage your product is in, based on the rate of sales growth, the level of sales expense, and the rate of profit.

Life-Cycle Stage	Rate of Sales Growth	Sales Expense	Profitability
Introduction	Slow	High	None
Growth	High	High	Low
Maturity	Moderate	Moderate	High
Decline	Slow	Low	Moderate*

*When profitability ceases, the product should be discontinued.

Using the matrix, you should be able to decide which of the four life-cycle stages your product is in. Next, use **Checklist 13,** Life-Cycle Expense Analysis, to estimate the cost of keeping the product as part of a direct marketing campaign through the rest of its life cycle.

7 Checklists for Conducting Marketing Research

The first piece of marketing research you should consider is to appraise the marketability of your product in terms of its potential strength in your market. Will the product sell better in one part of the country than another? Is it affected by the seasons? Will it be accepted by your customers? **Checklist 14,** Appraising a Product's Marketability, will help you answer these and myriad other questions.

If, using Checklist 14, you find that you are unable to answer various key questions about how the market will accept your product, you should consider conducting marketing research.

TYPES OF MARKETING RESEARCH YOU CAN CONDUCT

- **Concept Testing:** Determines value users place on product

- **Tracking Study:** Requires periodically contacting selected product users

- **Product Usage:** Determines present demand

- **Advertising Penetration:** Evaluates advertising message being used

- **Image Evaluation:** Helps determine strengths or weaknesses

- **Public Opinion Surveys:** Reveals customers' key issues

- **Copy Testing:** Ensures that advertising wording is appropriate for the target market

- **Test Marketing:** Tests consumer response to the product (e.g., at a shopping mall)

- **Product Placements:** Product is given to consumer for use at home

- **Test Marketing/Direct Mail:** Tests the potential response of an entire mailing list by mailing the sales offer to part of the list

- **Market Segmentation:** Determines how a market is segmented by product usage, demand, or customer profile (Can also learn demographic, psychographic, and product preference profiles by key market segments.)

- **Market Feasibility:** Analyzes potential demand for a new product or service, evaluates market size, and which market segments might be most receptive to the product

- **Market Share/Market Size:** Analyzes competitor's sales and industry sales of a product or product type

- **Competitive Analysis:** May be part of a market share study; evaluates competitors' strengths and weaknesses

- **Positioning:** Evaluates how consumers view company's or brand's image attributes

MARKET RESEARCH METHODS

There are two types of market research: *primary* and *secondary*. *Primary research* involves either contacting a portion of your target market population—in person, by telephone, by fax, by mail, or by computer—or observing them.

Secondary research involves getting information from printed sources or electronic databases.

Primary research may provide more current and precise data, but it can be expensive and time-consuming. Secondary research is usually faster and much less expensive, but it may not give you the specific information you are seeking. Secondary research resources can include sources that are internal and external to the company.

Internal Sources

- Files

- Reports

- Marketing information system (MIS) reports

- Sales and sales call reports

- Cost data

- Warranty cards

- Results of previous mail, space, or telemarketing campaigns

External Sources

- Libraries

- Government publications and reports

- Trade associations

- Universities

- Private research organizations

- Public and private databases

- Federal government departments

  1. Department of Commerce

  2. Federal Reserve Bank

- State government

- City government

- Banks

- Advertising agencies

- Mailing list brokers

Some Useful References

- *Encyclopedia of Associations*

- *The Statistical Abstract of the United States*

- *Business Periodicals Index*

- *The Yellow Pages*

- *Standard & Poor's Industry Surveys*

- *Standard Rate and Data Services* (SRDS)

- *Standard Industrial Classification (SIC) Manual*

CONDUCTING MARKET RESEARCH

Unless your target market is very small, it would make more sense in terms of cost and time to do your research with a group of customers who are representative of your target market rather than going to the entire target market. Therefore, researchers rarely contact their entire universe (take a census) but instead go to a *sample* of the population.

The advantages of sampling rather than taking a census include the following:

- Cost savings

- Time savings

- Ability to get in-depth information through focus groups, panels, personal interviews, telephone interviews, or mail surveys

- Less error (If a mistake is made, it is not made across the entire target market.)

- Greater practicality (If your target market was very large, you would probably not get to contact everyone.)

- Greater security (You can keep a new product secret much longer.)

- Greater accuracy (The fewer, more qualified people collecting the information, the better.)

Use **Checklist 15,** Sample Selection, as a starter for selecting a market sample.

PROBABILITY AND NONPROBABILITY SAMPLES

While there are several different types of samples, they fall into two distinct groups—probability and nonprobability samples.

The criteria for the *probability sample* is very specific and very strict. To be a probability sample, every member of the population that is the subject of your research must have the same *known chance* to be selected as part of the sample. *Known chance* refers to the degree of confidence in the accuracy of the sample truly representing the population. Degree of confidence measures the statistical accuracy of samples and is of limited use to most direct response marketers.

This example shows how nonprobability samples differ from probability samples. If you want to measure the opinions of the employees from a certain company about their health benefits and that company has offices in three separate locations, you decide to interview 200 people from the headquarters. To make the sample random, you select to talk to every eighth person leaving the building after 5 p.m. This is a *nonprobability sample,* since employees in the other two office locations do not have a chance to be selected.

Checklist 16, Diagnostic Questions to Determine Sample Size, will help you determine if a sample you are planning to use is a probability or nonprobability sample.

USING PROBABILITY AND NONPROBABILITY SAMPLES

If you need a true cross section of your market, you will need to select a *probability sample.* This method uses the element of chance, which means that anyone in your target population has an equal chance to be selected for the sample. Any sampling technique not involving chance is a *nonprobability sample.* Research methods of obtaining probability samples include the following:

1. **Random Number Generation:** Assign a number to each (and every) member of your target audience and select your sample using a table of random numbers.

2. **Stratified Sample:** Divide the total target market into subgroups and randomly select samples from each subgroup.

3. **Cluster Sample:** Divide the population into geographic subgroups such as neighborhoods and randomly select samples from the subgroups. This method is usually more efficient in terms of cost and time than a stratified sample for personal interviews.

4. **Systematic Samples:** Take a mailing list of names from the target population and randomly select the desired number of names. This is the method most used by direct marketers.

While not as statistically accurate, nonprobability samples are less expensive, less time-consuming, and easier to conduct than most probability samples. The most commonly used nonprobability samples are:

1. **Convenience Sample:** Select the members of the population closest at hand. This is the least expensive and time-consuming.

2. **Judgment Sample:** Have an expert in the field select members of each sample.

3. **Quota Sample:** Divide the target population into subgroups and select a certain number from each subgroup.

If you decide to use a nonprobability sample, here are some tips for getting consistently good samples:

- **Samples must be representative.** The sample should represent the target market. If you are using in-store interviews, try using the quota sample.

- **Be mindful of poor weather.** When people are in a hurry, they may want to get away from the interviewer as fast as possible and give quick and not necessarily accurate answers.

- **Avoid interviewer biases.** Interviewers may select only people they think they might like to talk to, rather than, for example, every fourth person leaving the store.

- **Avoid questions that require long explanations.** If the interviewer needs to explain the questions, respondents may not answer accurately.

- **Ask easy-to-answer questions first.** Personal questions about age and income should be asked late in the questionnaire; some respondents might object to them.

ESTIMATING RESEARCH COSTS

Printing and Mailing

Checklist 17, Estimating Research Costs: Printing and Mailing, will help you determine your budget for this project. The first line, preparation, refers to the costs of designing, typesetting, and preparing the camera-ready materials that will be used for printing. The third item, lists and directories, refers to the sources you will use to determine who will receive your questionnaire. If mailing lists are available, it may make sense to rent them; if they are not available, you may need to get appropriate directories and have the names selected from that source and then input into a database or simply typed on labels.

Mailing costs include the cost of inserting the questionnaire materials into envelopes and affixing postage. It is generally preferable to use first-class postage for research mailings. Recipients tend to open first-class letters right away whereas some people may ignore third class (bulk mailing) letters. If you do choose to use third class, you will save on postage but your mailing costs will increase since third class mailings need to be sorted by zip code and put into mailing bags.

Incentives often increase response, since you are rewarding the recipient for filling out your questionnaire. All the costs incurred for the incentive should be included. For example, if you include a dollar coin, it may have to be affixed to a letter or put into a small envelope or somehow prevented from moving around loose in the mailing envelope. There is a cost for each of these eventualities and that cost should be included in the cost of the mailing.

Operations

Checklist 18, Estimating Research Costs: Operations, itemizes all the costs involved with receiving, tabulating, and analyzing the results of your mailing. If you are conducting face-to-face or telephone interviews, you will want supervisors to work with your interviewers. They are available to make sure the interviewers are conducting the research properly and to answer questions the interviewers may have. If you are using computers to tabulate the data, you will need programmers to set up your database and coding clerks to transfer the data from the questionnaire into the computer. Report writers translate the data into a narrative format and report analysts interpret the data in terms of observations and recommendations the company can use in formulating an action plan. Make sure your cost estimates include all necessary research services.

SCHEDULING MARKETING RESEARCH

Checklist 19, Research Job Schedule, is a tool for anticipating and tracking the time spent on each phase of the research project. The columns indicate the number of hours spent, the dates of the beginning and ending of each phase, and the person responsible for supervising each phase. Working through this schedule will help you estimate costs and give you a sense of how long the entire project will take. Don't forget to allow time for the respondents to reply between the mail date and receipt of filled-out questionnaires.

Preliminary work refers to the time spent ascertaining just what information is being sought. This is a very critical stage for if you don't thoroughly understand the goal of the research, you can miss key information or collect irrelevant data. *Sample selection* involves finding names for the sample group and determining how the sample will be contacted. *Questionnaire creation* refers to determining the questions to be asked, the order in which they will be asked, and the design of the questionnaire so that it is easy to use and the results are easy to tabulate. *Printing and mailing* includes the creation of the questionnaire package and its delivery to the recipients and/or the interviewers. *Opening and sorting* are the operations involved when a mail questionnaire is returned. The envelopes must be opened and the questionnaires given to the coding clerk who inputs data (the respondents' answers) into a computer which must be programmed to receive, compile, and print out the data in a usable format.

The data on the printout is analyzed and a report is written. Clerical time is needed to type the report in final form, reproduce, and distribute it.

TIPS FOR PUTTING TOGETHER A RESEARCH PACKAGE

The Questionnaire

- The questionnaire should be easy to understand and fill out.

- The reader should feel that he or she is participating in an important and interesting project.

- Set up the answers so that they are easy to tabulate, compare, and analyze.

- The questions should be specific, not giving too much or too little information.

- Try not to word questions in such a way that the answers might be biased.

- Check to see that you have included all the important questions you want and that you eliminate those that are irrelevant.

- Pretest your questionnaire with a small group of customers *before* you go to press.

The Cover Letter

The cover letter should do the following:

- Be personal.

- Ask a favor.

- Stress the importance of responding.

- Assure the recipient that filling out the questionnaire is easy and will not take much time.

- Tell the recipient how he or she was chosen.

- Thank the recipient for responding and convey a sense of urgency.

- Describe the incentive—if you use one—and tell why it is being offered. (Adding the incentive as a P.S. will help increase your response rate.)

- Enclose a postage-paid reply envelope. Make sure it is big enough to hold the questionnaire.

The Envelope

The envelope should look as much as possible like a personal letter:

- Use a stamp, not an indicia. An *indicia* is a U.S. Postal Service marking used on bulk mailings that may prompt some recipients to perceive your mailing as "junk mail."

- Name and address typed or neatly handwritten.

When your research package is ready for mailing, double-check that you included all the necessary components using **Checklist 20**, Double-Checking Your Research Package.

4 Checklists for Forecasting Market Potential

Before beginning *any* new direct response campaign, it is essential to know exactly how profitable the campaign is likely to be. **Checklist 21,** Profit Planning, is one you may not be able to fill out right away, but make sure you complete it *before you spend any money on your campaign.* If you cannot answer all the questions in the checklist, you had better abandon or rethink your direct response campaign.

FORECASTING MARKET POTENTIAL

This section will give you in-depth help in forecasting the size of the market and how to reach it economically. **Checklist 22,** Preliminary Forecasting of Market Potential, will help you forecast market potential in primary, secondary, and other markets. For now, let's assume you've done the work and you know approximately how many prospects you can reach.

Consider the following questions:

1. How deeply do you think you can penetrate a market? For example, if you are selling something to architects and you find that there are approximately 60,000 of them reachable by direct response methods, how many do you think will eventually buy your product or service? Can you live with 5 percent or do you need 25 percent? Remember that market penetration is a long-term effort. You will not get 5 percent of the market with an initial effort.

2. How competitive is the market? Are other suppliers already entrenched selling similar items to this market? Will you have to get sales by wooing away customers from other suppliers, or is your product sufficiently unique that you can sell across the market? In other words, will the difference between your product and someone else's be immediately obvious to your prospect? If it will be obviously different or improved, your job of getting customers will be much easier.

3. Can you envision your product as part of a line that sells to a known and growing market, or is it geared to some current need or fad? For example, demographic studies show that the senior population will grow as a percentage of total population, and that they have more money than other age groups. Any product line you develop for this group should enjoy a growing, predictable market. On the other hand, consider the plight of the entrepreneurs who saw an opportunity to sell products or commemorative items relating to the Persian Gulf War. The

war ended quickly, public interest plummeted, and many were stuck with unsold inventory impossible to move at any price.

Forecasting Campaign Expenses and Profit Margins

Preliminary planning must include rough estimates of costs and margins available for selling expenses. Gross margin is gross profit. It refers to the amount of money you have left from sales (less returns) after you deduct the cost of the goods sold. A frequent cause of failure in the direct response marketplace is having too low a gross margin.

The following table is another way to explain gross margin:

	Gross Sales	
Less:	**Returns and Allowances**	Includes discounts and outside commissions
Equals:	**Net Sales**	Cash or accounts receivable
Less:	**Cost of Goods Sold**	The costs to manufacture the product
Equals:	**Gross Margin**	Can be expressed as a dollar amount or as a percentage of gross sales

Here is an example of figuring gross margin dollars for a single item:

	Net Price	$49.00
Less:	**Cost of Sales**	− 17.00
Equals:	**Gross Margin**	$32.00

To figure gross margin as a percentage, divide unit gross margin by the unit net price:

$$\frac{\text{Unit Gross Margin (\$)}}{\text{Unit Net Price (\$)}} = \frac{\$32}{\$49} = 65\%$$

Many managers selling in the direct response market only will consider selling products with a gross margin of more than 70 percent, so in the above example the 65 percent gross margin would be unacceptable. To raise the gross margin to 70 percent would require either raising the selling price or lowering the unit cost, as shown:

	Raise Selling Price	**Lower Unit Cost**
Price	$57.00	$49.00
Cost of goods sold	−17.00	−14.00
Gross margin	$40.00 (70%)	$35.00 (71%)

You will need a high gross margin if any of the following conditions apply:

1. **Selling costs are too high.** Direct response selling costs are generally higher than selling through other channels.

2. **Customer returns are high.** Remember, gross margin is figured after returns are credited.

3. **You are selling to customer lists other than your own.** Your own buyer lists are always more efficient to use than anyone else's for your products.

4. **You are introducing a new product or concept.**

5. **You have to recover high development costs.**

6. **The market is limited.**

7. **Bad debts or customer service costs are above average.**

You can live with a lower gross margin if any of the following conditions apply:

1. **The direct response operation is using existing overhead.**

2. **Selling costs are low.** If new product is shipped automatically to existing customers, sales costs will be minimal.

3. **The product (or company) enjoys customer recognition and loyalty.**

4. **You are selling exclusively to your own customer base.**

5. **Developmental costs are paid by other operations.**

6. **You are building a customer base for future sales.**

Checklist 23, Forecasting Expenses and Margins, will help you accurately forecast your expenses and profit margins.

Forecasting the Cost of Resourcees and Overhead

Direct response sales will not come without dedicating people and other resources to the job. However, this does not mean that you must immediately budget more for salaries and rent. For a start-up operation in direct response, you can engage an outside agency with agreed-on costs and schedules for results. The agreement should include a fair means of termination in case you want to bring the job in-house in the future. A direct response agency can handle all the creative and production functions of making a sale. A fulfillment house can also take care of specialized warehousing, billing, and shipping of your direct response product. However, a manager and some staff time will have to be allocated to supervise these functions.

IN A START-UP OPERATION, CONSIDER THE FOLLOWING OPTIONS:

1. Using outside direct response consultants for specialized knowledge.

2. Using free-lancers for creative work on ads, etc.

3. Using a fulfillment house experienced in direct response operations.

4. Looking at your competitors for ideas.

IN A START-UP OPERATION, AVOID THE FOLLOWING SITUATIONS:

1. Making expensive staff additions at the outset.

2. Imposing your creative ideas on experts you hire.

3. Assigning sales responsibility to non-sales oriented people.

4. Expecting success from the first test.

FORECASTING INCOME FROM SECONDARY SOURCES: A BY-PRODUCT OF DIRECT RESPONSE CAMPAIGNS

Direct response is unique in that it provides many opportunities to make money apart from selling your product. Often, this other income is sufficient to justify a break-even direct response operation in a company. Following are some secondary sources of profits for direct response companies:

- Income from renting customer and prospect names to non-competitors. The work of selling the names is handled by an outside list manager or broker; all you do is approve the rentals and cash the checks.

- Licensing or allowing others to sell your products via specialized catalogs.

- An "echo effect" in other sales operations. For example, a manufacturer of consumer goods enjoys sales increases in retail outlets after a direct mail campaign designed to generate mail-order sales.

When you are estimating your direct response revenue, don't omit these significant profit centers. For example, if you have a house list of 30,000 people who have purchased items from your company in the last two years, and you rent those names for $60 per thousand, each full rental of your list will gross about $1,800, less the broker's commission of 20 percent, for a net of $1,440. You may also have another 20,000 names of people who purchased items from your company more than two years ago (prior buyers). You may be able to rent these names for $40 per thousand, which would mean an additional $640 for the use of names of people who may have stopped buying from you. Here is $2,080 of income each time your full list is rented. You may decide that you will limit rentals to 10 times per year, so your incremental income from renting your lists would be $20,800.

Use **Checklist 24,** List Rental Profit Analysis, to help you assess the profitability of renting lists.

5 Checklists for Forecasting Sales

Estimating sales for a year or through the anticipated life of a product can be a little like gazing into a crystal ball. Whatever your sales estimates are, they are based on sets of assumptions about the future: your product will be accepted by the marketplace as you predict it will; there are no unforeseen local, national, or international economic changes that will affect sales; no new competing product will be introduced that will make your product obsolete, or any number of events beyond your control.

While sales estimating can be accomplished by your financial team based on the past history of similar products, the more input you can provide about your customers, the competition, the channels of distribution, and external forces, the more accurate your estimate is likely to be.

In this section we will deal with sales estimation across all channels of distribution and then focus on direct response sales estimation. We do this to put the direct response estimation in perspective and to show you the techniques other channels use so that you can better integrate your estimates with other members of the marketing team. Since direct response campaigns often influence sales through other channels, your having an understanding of the total sales estimating process could provide you with ammunition to show that direct response is a medium that is integral, not peripheral, to the sales process. In **Checklist 25,** Estimating Sales Across All Distribution Channels, for each channel used for the product or service under consideration, you will fill in the estimated number of units to be sold via that channel (Column A). Enter the price of the product or service in Column B. Then multiply Column A by Column B to derive an estimation of the revenue to be produced from each distribution channel.

METHODS FOR SALES ESTIMATING

1. **Executive Judgment:** Relies on informal analysis by management and uses personal knowledge of the industry as the basis for forecasting.

2 **Sales Force Surveys:** The sales force is in touch with customers, but they might have limited perspective or misinterpret consumer desires.

3. **Consumer Surveys:** Conducting surveys among consumers may show what the consumer *thinks* he or she might do, but consumers may, in fact, *act* differently.

Executive Judgment Forecasting

Use executive judgment forecasting under the following conditions:

1. When the executive(s) are experienced and have a good feel for the market and for customers' needs.

2. When you want to check on or fortify other methods of sales predictions.

3. When your budget for sales forecasting is limited.

4. When your company or product is new and sales data are not available.

5. When your sales volume is fairly stable and the market is well defined.

6. When the risk or consequences of serious error in forecasting is low.

Do not use executive judgment forecasting under the following conditions:

1. When it relies entirely on personal views and may be mostly guesswork.

2. When it provides no way of weighing and evaluating individual opinions.

3. When it may infringe too much on valuable executive time.

4. When in group forecasting, dominant individuals determine group opinion. Group pressure for conformity may discourage timid members.

5. When it tends to give equal weight to the predictions of the forecasters no matter how bad their estimates have been in the past.

6. When there is no established formula or methodology to follow, new executives could have difficulty in arriving at reasonable forecasts.

Sales Force Surveys

There are several problems associated with relying on sales force estimates.

1. Salespeople are usually poor estimators, especially when it comes to identifying long-term trends.

2. Current conditions are apt to color their forecasts; they are optimistic when sales are good and pessimistic when sales are declining.

3. Sales managers are usually so concerned with administrative problems that they don't keep up with national or international developments and trends that could affect their sales.

4. Salespeople may think it's smart to forecast low so their sales record looks good by comparison or forecast high to impress headquarters with their enthusiasm.

5. Sales force estimating is time-consuming; time might be better spent out in the field selling.

6. Salespeople are usually only interested in immediate results, so they may not give forecasting questionnaires enough thought.

Now use **Checklist 26,** Collecting Sales Estimates from Your Sales Force, to help determine the validity of sales estimates collected from your sales force.

Consumer Surveys

On the positive side, consumer surveys do the following;

1. Give a good feel of the market and its needs.

2. Keep you abreast of competition.

3. Provide clues to new products and new uses for existing products.

4. Indicate size of customer inventories.

5. Show where additional advertising, promotion, and personal selling pressures may be needed.

However, there are several disadvantages of using consumer surveys for forecasting:

1. Product users may be too numerous, or too hard and expensive to locate, even using a sample.

2. Many of those reached might not know, or be unwilling to reveal, their buying intentions. Or, having stated their intentions, they might change their minds about either purchase or time of purchase.

3. In the case of broad markets, the method requires very expert sampling, with repeated polling at frequent intervals to check changes in opinions or intentions.

4. Estimates based on customer surveys may be more a reflection of guesses by product users than informed judgment in the field.

5. Distributors and dealers may not be willing to take on the extra work of tracing and questioning customers or potential customers.

Estimating Sales Based on Sales History of Similar Products

Another method for estimating sales is by selecting other products that are similar in several ways—target market, price, and product usage—and factoring in price increases to arrive at a sales estimate.

ESTIMATING SALES FROM DIRECT RESPONSE CHANNELS

1. Identify similar products that have been sold through direct response channels.

2. Calculate the percentage of the total sale for each of the similar products sold through each direct response channel you plan to use.

3. Using the percentages from #2, above, apply those percentages as the basis for your new sales estimate.

4. Determine whether in-house buyers lists for your new product have increased or decreased and adjust your estimate accordingly.

5. Determine whether outside lists have increased or decreased and adjust your estimate accordingly.

6. Check the returns history for the in-house and outside lists and adjust your estimate accordingly.

7. Check the bad debts history for the in-house and outside lists and adjust your estimates accordingly.

TESTING LISTS TO ESTIMATE SALES

The more outside lists you test, the more risk you take, because you will probably have less information on the quality of the outside lists than you will have on your own. On the other hand, if you add few outside lists to your mailings, you will be adding fewer new names to your in-house buyers list and may run the risk of losing customers by attrition without replacing them.

List History

It is a good idea to keep a separate file on your experience with each outside list you use. **Checklist 27,** Tracking List History, will help you keep track of each list.

Guidelines for Testing New Lists

Examine each list that you plan to use and estimate your sales one list at a time and then aggregate them to get a total projected sales figure. If you are dealing with a brand-new list with which you have no experience, calculate and use your break-even point as your estimate. (See Appendix A for an explanation of calculating your break-even point.)

When testing new lists, you may find that of ten lists tested only four are worth retesting. Your overall response rate may be less than break-even because six of your ten lists failed. However, the purpose of testing is to weed out failures. You should avoid testing too many new lists at a time, because if more than half fail, your test results could kill a valid project.

The *echo effect* refers to the sales that are gained as a result of a direct response activity through another channel. In cases where a product is sold both through direct response and retail channels, there are many people who would rather purchase the product after having examined it for themselves instead of ordering it through the mail or by telephone.

When you use direct response among your sales channels, the echo effect should be anticipated and your sales estimates adjusted accordingly. There is no overall formula for estimating the incremental sales gained from the echo effect—it will vary from industry to industry and product type to product type.

If there are no accepted ratios for the echo effect in your industry, you may wish to test the echo effect for future estimating purposes. One method would be to take an existing product that is available in retail outlets, one that has not been supported through direct mail. If possible, wait until your retail sales for the product are beginning to decrease, then start your direct response campaign. As you track your retail orders (allowing for seasonal differences), you should see incremental sales for those products.

Checklist 28, Echo Effect Tracking, attempts to simplify a very complex concept. Since the echo effect is the incremental difference between a non-direct mail channel's normal sales activity and the sales generated as a result of a direct mail effort, you need to know what the normal sales of a particular channel were *before* the direct mail effort was made. In this checklist, we ask you to ascertain the average sales of the retail and *white mail* (miscellaneous orders that can't be tracked) channels for a period of six months before a direct-mail campaign was instituted. What we are seeking is an approximate percentage that can be applied to direct mail sales to estimate the effects of the campaign on these other sales channels. See the example on page 26.

Once you have selected the sales forecasting method or methods appropriate for your needs, double-check that you have considered all the points on **Checklist 29,** Double-Checking Sales Forecasts.

An Example of
Estimating the Echo
Effect

Product: _____

Activity	Month 1 results	Month 2 results	Month 3 results	3 month average
Direct response sales	200	150	100	150
Average retail sales (6 months prior)	100	100	100	100
Average "white mail" sale (6 months prior)	20	20	20	20
Total average retail and white mail	120	120	120	120
Retail actual	140	130	120	130
White mail actual	30	25	20	25
Total retail and white mail actual	170	155	140	155
Incremental sales increase	50	35	20	35

Echo effect % = Incremental sales increase ÷ direct response sales (35 ÷ 150 = 23.3%).

Therefore, for every $100 in direct mail sales, an additional $23.30 is generated by the echo effect.

CHECKLIST 1   Direct Response Goals Worksheet

A = Most important

B = Very important

C = Moderately important

D = Slightly important

E = Not important

	Goal	A	B	C	D	E
1	Increase profits					
2	Increase sales					
3	Build mailing lists for internal use					
4	Build mailing lists for rental					
5	Segment target market					
6	Support field sales force					
7	Price testing					
8	Support wholesalers					
9	Support dealers					
10	Market testing					
11	New product development					
12	New product testing					
13	Develop international markets					
14	Market research					
15	Increase internal resource efficiencies					
16	Other					

CHECKLIST 2 Setting and Prioritizing Goals

Rank	Goal	Due Date
1		
2		
3		
4		
5		

CHECKLIST 3 Quantifying Marketing Objectives

Marketing Goal	Percentage or Dollar Objective	Due Date	Approval Obtained
1			
2			
3			
4			
5			
6			
7			
8			
9			

CHECKLIST 4 Verifying Product Suitability for Direct Response Sales

	Yes	No	Comments
1. Is this product one that customers could buy elsewhere?			
2. Do you intend to charge a similar price to other outlets?			
3. Is your source of supply for this product dependable?			
4. Do you require special packaging for shipment?			
5. Does the item require special handling in warehousing and shipment? (Is it fragile or perishable?)			
6. Will you be able to sell other, related products to purchasers of this product?			
7. Are mailing lists and other direct response media available to reach the target market?			
8. Does the product fit in with the rest of your line? (Quality, market, customer perception)			
9. Is this a fad product with a limited life?			
10. Are returned products reusable?			
11. Will you be responsible for honoring guarantees or warranties?			
12. Are there special government regulations you will have to observe?			

CHECKLIST 5 Determining Product Attributes and Benefits

Product Attribute	Benefit to Customer
1.	
2.	
3.	
4.	
5.	
6.	

CHECKLIST 6   Establishing Target Market Profiles

I.   Demographics

Description	Unit Sales	Sales ($)	Percentage of Total
Age:			
Under 18			
18–29			
30–39			
40–49			
50–64			
65 and over			
Gender:			
Male			
Female			
Income:			
Up to $15,000			
$15,000–25,000			
$26,000–40,000			
$41,000–55,000			
$56,000–75,000			
Over $75,000			
Education:			
8th grade			
High school diploma			
Some college			
College degree			
Graduate degree			

II. Psychographics

Description	Unit Sales	Sales ($)	Percentage of Total
Frequency of Use:			
1 time			
2 times			
3 times			
4 or more times			
Competitive Brands Purchased:			
A.			
B.			
C.			
D.			
Method of Payment:			
Cash/check			
VISA/MasterCard			
American Express			
Other credit card			
Money order			
Other:			

CHECKLIST 6   (*Continued*)

III. Location

Location	Units Sold	Sales ($)	Percentage of Total
Northeast			
Mid-Atlantic			
Southeast			
North Central			
Mid-Central			
South Central			
Rocky Mountain			
Northwest			
West			
Southwest			
Totals:			

Target Market Segments	Size of Segment	Comments
1.		
2.		
3.		
4.		
5.		
6.		
7.		
8.		
Total Target Market:		

A	B	C	D
Segment	Additional Cost Required	Maximum Sales Increase	Pursue or Abandon?

CHECKLIST 9   Quantifying Marketing Objectives by Target Market Segment

Segment Name	Segment Size	Units Sold	Unit Price	Revenue
1.				
2.				
3.				
4.				
5.				
6.				
7.				
8.				
9.				
10.				
Totals:				

CHECKLIST 10   Calculating The Cost of Educating Customers

Customer Education Expenses	Cost ($)	Time
Professional media press releases		
Consumer media press releases		
Press conferences		
Media events		
Testimonials		
Professional reviews		
Professional free samples		
Other:		
Totals:		

Price Variables	Sales (Units)	Sales ($)	Cost of Goods Sold	Gross Profit
Price A:				
Price B:				
Price C:				
Price D:				
Price E:				
Price F:				

CHECKLIST 12 Competitive Price Comparison

	1	2	3	4
	Your Price[a]	Competitor's Price[b]	Price Differential[c]	Customer Acceptance[d]
A.				
B.				
C.				
D.				
E.				
F.				

[a]The price to the customer for the product (all rows use same price)

[b]Each row is a different competitor's price to the customer.

[c]Column 1 - Column 2. This may be a positive number (if your price is higher than your competitor's) or a negative number (if your price is lower than your competitor's).

[d]How the customer perceives the price differential between your price and your competitors': **Fair, Somewhat High, Very high, Somewhat low, Very low.**

CHECKLIST 13   Life-Cycle Expense Analysis

Introductory Stage

Activity	Budgeted Expense	Actual Expense
Space ads		
Newspaper ads		
Direct mail		
Telemarketing		
Sales promotion		
Trade shows		
Catalogs		
Publicity		
Other		

Growth Stage

Activity	Budgeted Expense	Actual Expense
Space ads		
Newspaper ads		
Direct mail		
Telemarketing		
Sales promotion		
Trade shows		
Catalogs		
Publicity		
Other		

Maturity Stage

Activity	Budgeted Expense	Actual Expense
Space ads		
Newspaper ads		
Direct mail		
Telemarketing		
Sales promotion		
Trade shows		
Catalogs		
Publicity		
Other		

Decline Stage

Activity	Budgeted Expense	Actual Expense
Space ads		
Newspaper ads		
Direct mail		
Telemarketing		
Sales promotion		
Trade shows		
Catalogs		
Publicity		
Other		

CHECKLIST 14   Appraising a Product's Marketability

I. **Strength of Market (For each market, rank, *Weak, Moderate,* or *Strong.*)**

	National	Regional	Local
Growth potential			
Acceptance of price levels			
Company position			
Export possibilities			
Seasonality			

CHECKLIST 14 (*Continued*)

II. Acceptance

	Yes/No	Comments
Does product supplement existing company product?		
Will customers recognize differentiation?		
Could product become a commodity?		
If yes, are you prepared to compete on the basis of:		
Price?		
Level of service?		
Sales promotion?		

III. Competition

	Yes/No	Comments
Does product have direct competition?		
Are customers fiercely loyal to competition?		

Competitors	Strong	Moderate	Weak	Comments
A.				
B.				
C.				
D.				

CHECKLIST 15 Sample Selection

Defining the target population

☐ Consumer   ☐ Business

Indicate applicable parameters for interviewing

Consumers

Individuals	Age	Income	Gender	Education	Prod. User	Geo. Location	Other
at home							
at work							
shopping							
leisure							
Households							

Business

Relationship to Purchase Decision	Company Size	Position	Prod. User	Prod. Pros.	Geo. Location	Other
Decision Makers						
Specifiers						
Influencers						

CHECKLIST 16   Diagnostic Questions to Determine Sample Type

(A *no* answer for #1–3 or a *yes* answer for #4–6 identifies the sample as *nonprobability*)

Sample Selection	Yes	No	Comments
1. Does the sample you plan to use truly represent the population you wish to interview?			
2. Is most of the population accessible to you? (95% or more)			
3. Is your selection method mathematically random?			
4. Did you select the sample based on proximity to your office or the office of your interviewers?			
5. Is your sample comprised of people whom you feel are experts in the subject about which you are seeking information?			
6. Do you allow your interviewers to ignore certain members of a sample because of the physical characteristics of those people?			

CHECKLIST 17   Estimating Research Costs: Printing and Mailing

Research Title: _____ Date:_____

Number Mailed:_____

Printing and Mailing Costs: _____

Preparation $ _____

Printing $ _____

Lists and Directories $ _____

Mailing $ _____

Postage $ _____

Incentives $ _____

Total Printing and Mailing Costs: $ _____

Personnel	Estimated Hours	Rate per hour ($)	Total ($)
Supervisors			
Interviewers			
Computer programmers			
Coding clerks			
Report writers			
Proofreaders			
Report analysts			
Totals:			

CHECKLIST 19　Research Job Schedule

Research Title: _____　Date:_____

Date Due:_____　Mail Date: _____

Operations	Hours	From	To	Supervisor
Preliminary work				
Sample selection				
Questionnaire creation				
Printing and mailing				
Opening and sorting				
Computer programming				
Data input				
Data generation				
Data analysis				
Report writing				
Typing and processing				

Make sure your package includes a:	✔
Cover letter	
Incentive for completing the questionnaire	
Envelope:	
Stamped	
Hand addressed	
Typed	
Questionnaire	
Postage-paid reply envelope	
Postage-paid reply card (to request incentive)	

	✔ or Quantity	Comments
1. Can you identify the tarket market?		
2. Can you locate your target market?		
3. What is the size of your target market?		
4. How many units must you sell to break even?		
5. What percentage of the target market does the break-even point represent?		
6. What is your profit goal for this campaign?		
7. How many units must you sell to realize the profit goal?		
8. What percentage of the target market does the profit goal represent?		
9. Are the percentages in #5 and #8 above realistic?		

CHECKLIST 22   Preliminary Forecasting of Market Potential

Product: _____ Code: _____ Price: _____

Market	Size of Market (000s)	Information Source	Estimated Market Penetration (%)	Estimate of Units Sold	Estimated Revenue
Primary Markets: 1.					
2.					
3.					
4.					

Secondary Markets: 1.					
2.					
3.					
4.					

Other: 1.					
2.					
3.					
4.					

Sales Estimates ($000s) (Highest to Lowest)	Estimated Unit Price	Estimated Unit Cost	Gross Margin	Overhead (%)	Overhead ($)	Contribution to Profit

CHECKLIST 24   List Rental Profit Analysis

List Name _____

Total Number of Names: _____   Date of Last Update: _____

Number of Hotline Names: _____ Number of Regular Names: _____ Number of Prior Names: _____ Number of Inquiry Names: _____

A List	B Rental rate per thousand	C Estimated number of names rented per year (000s)	D Estimated annual revenue	E Broker's commission	F Label expenses	G Net profit
Hot-line names (up to 90 days)						
Regular names (90–days to 2 years)						
Prior names (over 2 years)						
Inquiries and non-buyers						
Totals						

Column D = Column B × Column C

Column G = Column D – Column E – Column F

CHECKLIST 25 Estimating Sales Across All Distribution Channels

Channel Name	A Units Sold	B Unit Price	C Revenue[a]
1. Direct mail			
2. Premium			
3. Retail			
4. Space advertising			
5. Special market			
6. Special sale			
7. Telemarketing, inbound			
8. Telemarketing, outbound			
9. Trade show			
10. White mail			
11. Wholesale			
12. Other			
Totals:			

[a]Column A × Column B.

	Yes	No
1. Has past experience shown that estimates by your sales force personnel are reliable?		
2. Since some salespeople tend to overestimate and others to underestimate, do you keep a record of their accuracy in the past and adjust their estimates accordingly?		
3. Do you provide salespeople with data to help them forecast, such as sales by product or customer for the year to date and for recent past years?		
4. Do you have a form for salespeople to use in making their estimates?		
5. Is the form uniform among all districts?		
6. Is company policy made clear, such as that estimates should be made on the basis of existing product or service lines and current price structure with no speculation as to product or price changes?		
7. Is it made clear to the salespeople that their quotas will not necessarily be based on their estimates, to offset the obvious possibilities of bias?		

List History for: Source: Date List Last Used:_____	Quantity or Percentage	Positive (✔) or Negative (–) Flag
Total quantity available		
Cost per thousand (CPM)		
Quantity of Names used		
Gross orders ($ Value)		
Response (%)		
Number of bad debts		
Percentage of bad debts ($ Value)		
Number of items returned		
Percentage of items returned ($ Value)		
Net orders ($ value)		

Activity	Month 1 results	Month 2 results	Month 3 results	3 month average
Direct response sales				
Average retail sales (6 months prior)				
Average "white mail" sale (6 months prior)				
Total average retail and white mail				
Retail actual				
White mail actual				
Total retail and white mail actual				
Incremental sales increase				

Echo effect % = Incremental sales increase ÷ direct response sales

	Yes	No	Comments
1. Are my facts and figures reliable by past experience?			
2. Am I using all the data available from outside sources: trade associations and publications, Census Bureau, etc?			
3. Am I basing my forecast on at least two years' worth of data?			
4. When I feel that the forecast figures aren't right, do I trust my experience and understanding of the market?			
5. Do I encourage judgment contributions from my associates?			
6. Do I revise my forecasts as new data is received?			
7. Am I using more than one forecasting method for greater reliability?			
8. Do I avoid vague generalities?			
9. Do I give my assumptions and tell how I arrived at them?			
10. Do I give a range of error? (Pinpoint accuracy in sales forecasting is often accidental.)			

PART II
Using the Direct Marketing Media

■ *7 Checklists for Media Planning*

■ *11 Checklists for Direct Mail and Mailing Lists*

■ *4 Checklists for Space Advertising*

■ *12 Checklists for Catalogs*

■ *10 Checklists for Card Packs and Package Inserts*

■ *7 Checklists for Telemarketing*

7 Checklists
for Media Planning

Media are the means by which you communicate your message to your prospect or customer. They include direct mail, space advertising in magazines and newspapers, radio and television, and every other means of public communication. While virtually every type of media can be used for direct response, some are used so frequently for this purpose that we tend to think of them first in any discussion of direct response.

Some common direct response media include the following:

1. **Direct mail:** Letters, catalogs, and solo or package mailings (either personalized with the recipient's name or nonpersonalized bulk mail)

2. **Space ads:**

    A. Magazines

    B. Newspapers

    C. Professional journals

    D. Directories and other specialized books

3. **Alternative print media:** Card packs and postcards in catalogs; inserts in packages; mailing postcards and coupons distributed with products and in stores; and freestanding inserts in newspapers

4. **Radio and TV commercials:** Toll-free (800) numbers or toll-call (900) numbers

5. **TV infomercials:** Half-hour TV programs that concentrate on selling a particular product or line of products

SELECTING MEDIA

Even before you think about costs, circulation, and other nitty-gritty details, every media suggestion or choice should be checked against **Checklist 30,** a Four-Point Media Checklist. Make sure that for each medium you plan to use you can answer *yes* to all four questions. If you cannot confidently answer *yes,* research that medium further before you include it in your media plan.

COMPARING MEDIA

All direct response media can be compared in terms of expected response. In other words, your potential customers can be classified into *primary markets, secondary markets,* and even *tertiary markets.* It is important in your media analysis to differentiate among these various markets. For example, assume that you are responsible for marketing a construction handbook. Your market analysis might look like the following:

Primary Markets	Estimate of Unit Sales	Secondary Markets	Estimate of Unit Sales	Tertiary Markets	Estimate of Unit Sales
Contractors	10,000	Trade school teachers	2,000	Students	200
Construction superintendents	7,500	Professors of construction engineering	1,000	International markets	600
Architects and design engineers	5,000	Libraries	800	Technicians	100
Cost estimators	3,500				

As you can see from this chart, the tertiary markets are real but relatively small. Is it worthwhile, for example, to pursue sales to technicians when the potential is only 100 copies? If this handbook sells for more than $100 and your potential sales are $10,000, an inexpensive ad in a technical magazine may be a good test—much depends on the resources you have at your disposal. You need to have a good idea of where your sales will come from and how significant secondary and tertiary market sales will be in meeting your sales goals.

All your media decisions will be based on your analysis of the various markets and their importance. In fact, sales and expense budgets should be segregated by market, because selling to secondary and tertiary markets is generally more expensive than selling to your primary or target market.

Before you decide on specific media, you will want a good estimate of the total audience universe available to you and what your sales expectations are from each audience segment. You will get your best response from your primary market and less response from secondary and tertiary markets. Your spending decisions will always come down to answering the question, "How much will it cost me to reach this segment, and what are reasonable sales expectations?"

If several media reach your target market, you will probably want to select those that have the greatest potential for selling your product. **Checklist 31,** Media Comparison Chart, will help you analyze various media by helping you discover what percentage of each medium's total circulation consists of the audience you intend to target. To be classified as primary media, more than half the audience should be in your target market. Sometimes no magazine, publication, list, TV channel, etc., has more than half its audience as your target market. In those cases, adjust the required percentages based on the realities of the available media.

For example, suppose you intend to sell electronic equipment for use in college physics laboratories. You place a direct response advertisement in a journal whose total circulation is 10,000 subscribers. The readers of the journal are categorized as 57 percent college physics instructors, 34 percent laboratory assistants, and 9 percent research physicists. Therefore, your primary audience is the 5,700 physics instructors.

A *secondary audience* is a minor segment of the target market. If the primary audience is between 50 percent and 60 percent, a 30 percent secondary audience is the minimum portion of the total circulation you should accept to use a magazine. The 3,400 laboratory assistants in the previous example (34 percent of circulation) represent your secondary audience. In some cases, only a small percentage of a medium's audience may be in your target market, but if it is the only medium that *does* reach that market, you may want to consider using it, despite the low percentage.

Once you have determined which are your primary, secondary, and tertiary media, you should rank them. **Checklist 32,** Media Ranking Chart, will help you decide which media to use and which to eliminate.

After you have selected and ranked the media most likely to reach your targeted market segments, you will need to establish a media calendar to plan the direct response efforts you will make for the year. **Checklist 33,** Media Calendar, will assist you with this scheduling. Many elements must be considered in this process. For example, Yellow Pages telephone directories are usually published just once a year; you must be aware of their copy deadlines. In the previous example of electronic laboratory equipment, you would need to place the advertisement at the time of year when college budgets for the year are being reviewed.

USING MEDIA TO GENERATE LEADS

All media can be sources of leads for your telemarketing and/or field sales force or for direct mail follow-up. When someone responds to an ad you have placed in a magazine, for example, make sure you keep a record of the inquiry. You should qualify *all* inquiries, as any one of them may represent a potential sale.

One technique to help qualify a lead is to ask the prospect to make an effort to get more information from your company. Depending on your objectives, you may require a prospect to fill out a coupon, place it in his or her own envelope and pay the postage back to you. Some insert cards do not carry prepaid postage indicias, so the prospect must furnish a stamp. The theory here is that only people who are really interested in your product will be willing to expend much effort to get more information. In contrast to this method of qualifying leads is the use of bingo cards (or reader service cards). These cards are usually bound into magazines, and readers simply circle the numbers that correspond to products advertised in the magazine and drop the card in a mailbox. Bingo cards require no expense and minimal effort from the prospect and therefore are considered unqualified leads.

Use **Checklist 34,** Lead Generation by Sales Representative, to keep track of leads from each medium and which representative responded to those leads.

Checklist 35, Tracking Leads, will help you keep track of the total number of leads you have sent to each representative, by week. If certain representatives are not receiving as many leads as some others, you may want to check on the geographic reach of the media you are using. Sales management will probably find this checklist useful as well.

Checklist 36, Estimating Media Reach to Generate Leads, helps you track the number of leads the advertising department is sending to company sales representatives. Here is a hypothetical example of how this checklist works.

Sales Representative Sallee Green works for a company that sells burglar alarms. While Sallee does some prospecting on her own, she needs a constant supply of names of people who are genuinely interested in home protection and have the money to purchase a system from her company. Leads are generated by people sending in coupons and calling an 800 number in response to advertising. Sallee can make four sales calls a day and therefore needs 20 leads a week or about 80 per month. Since Sallee is one of 20 other sales people, your job is to generate 1,600 sales leads per month.

You will build up a history of the kind of response you can anticipate from each media you use to generate leads and you will also build a history of how many of those leads are people who are genuinely interested and can afford to buy a burglar alarm system for their home. You might have a telemarketing operation seeking leads and/or qualifying the prospects who have responded to advertising. A capable telemarketer should be able to weed out people who are curious about your product or may be vaguely interested but are not sufficiently qualified to have a sales representative call at this time.

The difference between the average percentage of qualified leads and the actual number of qualified leads in Checklist 35 is a reality check to help you refine your qualified lead percentages for each media. Getting the information for the actual number of qualified leads requires feedback from the representatives. It is in everyone's best interest to know which advertisements in which media generate the best leads.

11 Checklists for Direct Mail and Mailing Lists

Direct mail decisions and list decisions go hand in hand. Without suitable lists, a successful direct mail campaign is impossible. The size and quality of the lists available should be considered when making a decision to do a mail campaign. If you have difficulty in locating promising lists to test, you should consider reaching your audience through other media.

RATING LISTS

There are many choices available when you finally decide to pick a dozen or so lists for a test. You should start with the most promising lists available and test outwardly from this core market. If "good" lists don't work, marginal lists certainly won't do any better. Here is a 1-to-10 rating scale that will help you make sounder decisions; a list rated 10 is the best, and 1 is the worst.

BEST—
Scale of 10

The best list in the world is your own list of previous direct mail customers. It is unfortunate that many mail-order companies fail to keep this list in top-notch condition. Your customer file should be segmented in such ways that you can reach them by recency or frequency of purchase, type of products purchased, payment records, dollar amount spent within a certain period, credit card history, and the like. This is the first list to test with any new campaign or product.

VERY GOOD—
Scale of 9 to 8

Inquiry names you have generated by advertising in other media are next best after your own lists. If you don't have a customer file to mail to, it is often productive to run ads to generate inquiries that you can use later as a mailing list. Inquiry lists are good because the person asking for information most likely was attracted to the ad, then had to get paper, an envelope, and a stamp, and finally write and mail the inquiry. This suggests a serious interest in your offer.

GOOD—
Scale of 7 to 6

You will work with your list broker to get recommendations for lists in this category. Generally speaking, these are mail-order buyers of products related to the one you are selling. The closer the product purchased is to the one you are offering, the better the chance of making a sale. A buyer of a business book from one publisher is an ideal prospect for a noncompeting book from another business publisher. A subscriber to a business magazine might be rated slightly lower, because magazine readers are not necessarily book buyers.

**FAIR TO POOR—
Scale of 5 to 3**

This is the risky part of direct mail list selection. The lists falling into this category are often compiled from public records, telephone Yellow Pages, directories, and similar sources. Some of these lists can be used to generate inquiries that are later used for direct mail campaigns. Raw lists of names with no other information are probably the least likely to succeed and should be avoided.

However, with some "tinkering" you can upgrade some lists. For example, if you're selling bookkeeping supplies to small businesses you can improve response by doing two things. First, have your list manager sort out smaller businesses from the large, general universe of names. Second, even though you may not have a personal name available, you can address the letter to "Chief Bookkeeper" to ensure delivery to a likely prospect. Just mailing your offer across the board to all businesses would result in certain failure.

**VERY POOR—
Scale of 2 to 1**

Any list with a poor pedigree should be dismissed from your decision making at once. These are lists that come from uncertain sources, are poorly maintained and filled with undeliverable names and addresses, are two or more years old, or are generated from non–direct response sources. Beware of any list that is a conglomeration of smaller lists. Apart from costly duplication of names, the lists usually have no relation to one another. Often, they are offered at bargain rates.

MANAGING LISTS

Lists are crucial to the success of a direct-response operation and most companies find it necessary and profitable to hire an inside list manager. He or she is usually responsible for:

- Customer list management, including systems for adding new names, updating files, deleting old names and bad debt names, running lists for exchange or rental with outside firms, and similar duties;

- Negotiating with outside brokers and list owners, keeping aware of new lists reaching the market, and being a source of list information to marketing managers;

- Handling the record keeping so essential for good list management, including details on lists used, results, list history, and so on.

Lacking an in-house list manager, the marketing manager has to assume many of these functions. The best source of list information is a list broker and you should use his or her services to the fullest. Other jobs are made easier with the help of Checklists 37, 38, 39, and 40. Let's take a look at each.

Checklist 37, Selecting Mailing Lists, is a useful tracking device, if the lists you use are relatively small and you plan to use all the segments making up the list. An example might be if you plan to promote an all-inclusive handbook to a professional group where you feel all the members of the group would be interested in the product.

Checklist 38, Sources of Names per Segment, is useful if the lists you select are large and you plan to use only portions or segments of the list to promote your product. Often, subscriber lists of magazines are segmented in great detail. Remember: the more segmentation you request, the higher the response, but at greater cost.

Checklist 39, List Rental Form, can be used to request lists for a campaign from your in-house list manager or made part of a rental order sent to a list broker. It is important at this stage to give deadlines. Also, remember that the list should be delivered to your lettershop in ample time to make the mail date.

Checklist 40, List Performance Analysis, provides vital information on the performance of lists. By tracking actual responses from a sample from the list against your performance goal, you know whether to mail to the remaining names on the list. Over a period of time, such a list history will tell you which lists are generally "hot" and which are disappointing. Future tests can avoid these poor performing lists to save money.

CREATING DIRECT MAIL PIECES

If you've carried out a careful analysis of your product and its pricing structure, its market potential, and lists available and have an idea of what to spend on the campaign, you are ready to schedule a mailing. Your campaign decision might range from a postcard in a card pack to an elaborate full-color brochure with personalized letters and order forms. There is no substitute for judgment in this area. With experience you will know what kind of sales will justify a given campaign. Part III, which covers direct marketing formats, copy, and art, will give you additional insights into when to use what formats.

A direct mail campaign consists of many elements; some easy way to track them is needed. **Checklist 41,** Components of a Direct Response Campaign, covers the important elements. You can add additional lines for special components you may decide to include. The important thing to remember is that a direct mail campaign is like a pyramid of efforts, all converging to a single point—your mail date. Give yourself plenty of time to create the copy and art and get all the necessary approvals.

Checklist 42, Campaign Schedule, will help you juggle all the details of the mailing, but you have to be assiduous in making all the entries and keeping on top of various deadlines. Some marketing managers like to keep a form like this in a day book and refer to it constantly. Others like to put this information on a large calendar or scheduling board so it is constantly in view.

It is important to plan far enough ahead to allow all the pieces to come together without crisis deadlines. Allow enough time for the creative process and all the approvals needed. Outside lists take time because you often have to submit samples before getting permission to use the lists.

One easy way to use this checklist to discover how long it takes to do a job from start to finish is to fill in the dates in reverse order—from the bottom up. Start with a desired mail date, and then work backwards, allowing time for each step. You will get a much more realistic estimate of the time involved if you do it this way.

CAMPAIGN ANALYSIS

The direct mail manager is constantly looking at orders, returns, bad debts, and other campaign results to see if a particular campaign can be expanded to the rest of the test lists or to other, yet untested, lists. Keep track of these elements on **Checklist 43,** Analyzing the Direct Mail Campaign. This will help you decide which lists are working and which should be dropped. Equally important, it will enable you to project future income and profits, because you now know how the tests have worked.

ELEMENTS OF A SUCCESSFUL MAIL CAMPAIGN

- Every dollar spent on a campaign should bring in several dollars in additional revenue. Do not add anything to a campaign simply to make it "look good" unless it will increase sales.

- Explore in advance how much time you need to create the mailing package, get it printed, and delivered to the mailing house. Then allow additional time for unforeseen delays.

- Leave plenty of time for ordering lists, getting approvals, and delivering the lists to the mailing house. Remember, many list owners run their list rentals at the same time they update their lists; that can be once a month.

The creative aspects of a direct mail campaign are vital to the success of the campaign, but poor execution can ruin the best creative job. If a mailing is sent to poorly chosen lists, if the various elements languish at the printer's or the mailing house warehouse, if important details like list format are overlooked, much time will be wasted. Often, this means your product sits in your warehouse eating up investment capital while your mailing waits for some small element before it can be mailed.

PLANNING FOR THE FUTURE

No business will last for very long without a planned growth strategy. This is especially true in direct response marketing, because response to your offers will taper off as you go back to the same prospects with the same offer or product. Unlike a successful retail business, which can open branches in other locations, mailing lists and other direct response media are limiting factors when it comes to reaching new customers.

In addition, by their very nature, direct response successes encourage competition. The more pieces you mail, or the more ads you place, the more people will see what you are doing. Among the prospects you reach will be potential competitors. Therefore, you have to make a plan to grow if you want to stay in business long.

This section asks you to consider the following types of goals:

- Short-range: the next 12 months

- Mid-range: 2 to 3 years ahead

- Long-range: 4 to 5 years ahead

Planning future goals is a crucial part of business, even though you know that many of your predictions will involve educated guesses. Often your guesses or estimates will cancel out and the bottom line will come out close to your predictions. The whole job is made easier, and more accurate, if you look at various segments of your business that contribute to growth. This is more realistic than simply "guessing" at a sales figure for each of the five years in advance. **Checklist 44**, Predicting Growth Areas, should be used as a starting point; your own business will suggest what other "growth areas" should be examined.

Product Lines

If you already produce a number of new products each year, you have a history of growth that can be examined. In looking at this growth area, consider the following:

1. Can the number of new products introduced each year be increased without adding to overhead? If not, then make allowances for new machines, personnel, and so on.

2. Be realistic about product lifetimes. If sales are decreasing, don't try to maintain a previous year's sales figure unless you're willing to invest more in marketing an old product.

3. Be aware that not all new products will be successful and meet their sales estimates; allow for failures.

Tracking the Competition

Checklist 45, Tracking the Competition, involves getting as much information as you can about your competitors. If your competitors are publicly held companies, you can get an annual report, which may give you some of the information you are seeking, but intelligence gathering on competition involves many additional sources. You should have some way for your sales representatives to keep you informed about what your competitors are doing in the field. You should get on the competitions' mailing lists. This might involve buying some products—sent to your home address—or ordering and then returning products. You will be interested in their packaging, response times, customer service practices, their courtesy toward customers, or any number of different aspects of their operation. You will probably want to keep a file on space ads and mailings by competitors, and you may ask selected sales representatives to check key competitors' booths (even take photos of them) at important trade shows.

Outside Mailing Lists

In any direct response sales effort, prime lists are quickly used up, unless the offer appeals to a market that is continually renewing itself (e.g., newly married couples, college graduates, self-improvement prospects, etc.). Consider the following when you try to estimate list usage:

1. Is this a list that is refreshed with new names every year, or is the basic list fairly static? For example, if you sell to civil engineers, you will find that the total number of names varies little; small drop-offs due to retirement and other reasons are balanced by small additions of new graduates. If the list is static, you can't mail as frequently because the same people keep getting your message, and it may lose some effectiveness.

2. Mailing list usage should grow proportionately to the new products introduced and should decrease as you drop products from the line. If the total product line grows, then mailing list usage should grow also.

3. Have you explored all sources of new lists to test? Here is where a competent list broker can help you discover new lists to test or suggest ways of improving current list usage. If you make many list segmentations, costs will go up, but response should also improve.

Use **Checklist 46**, Mailing List Broker Data, to keep records on lists and brokers you use.

Media

Here you should put all current media and costs. Then estimate what you will need to promote the new products and whether you will expand media to include things you may not have used before. Don't overestimate the response from new media; it is better to be conservative in estimates until you have some experience in new areas, such as card packs or inserts.

Telemarketing

All signs point to growth in this direct response medium, and you should plan for it regardless of your product line. Like direct mail, a telephone can generate orders and inquiries for any type of product or service. If you do not have a telemarketing operation, consider using an outside telemarketing service before adding in-house overhead in this area.

New Marketing Technologies

Although it is perhaps not appropriate as a short-term goal, you should assume that you will be using a new form of marketing to some degree within a few years. You will be guessing in this area, but a guess is better than ignoring the concept entirely. Your competitors certainly will not be ignoring new marketing avenues. Some of what you may consider technologies of the future may already be used by some of your competitors. If so, you should be testing them. Being first in a new technology isn't always critical—and for technologies that don't pan out, not being first will save time and money—but are you looking into infomercials, for example? Will the electronic kiosk turn into a valued in-the-mall direct response sales vehicle for you? Will the advent of CD-ROM and touchscreen technology mean a whole new world of opportunity and expense? Are you experimenting with computer networks? Many merchants and manufacturers sell directly to individuals worldwide through CompuServe and Prodigy. If information is your product, why not package it in discrete units and make it available via a 900 number? The possibilities of new technologies seem endless.

Gross Margins   You should constantly strive to improve your gross margins. This means investment in cost-cutting equipment; adopting new technologies for production; material substitutions; and any other measures that can produce your product more efficiently and at less cost.

Coupled with cost cutting should be a plan to raise prices in line with other prices in the market and to reflect the cost of materials going into your product. This is a very tricky area, because you can price yourself out of the market if you do not examine each increase carefully.

Use **Checklist 47,** Price Analysis, to help you evaluate current—and future—pricing practices.

Now you can get to the important matter of forecasting sales, marketing expenses, personnel requirements, overhead, and profit for the next several years. While still a guess, the numbers you have used in Checklist 43 should give you guidance in estimating. For example, sales and marketing expenses should rise together. If marketing expenses rise less steeply than sales, so much the better, but be realistic in the percentage improvement you can achieve. Don't expect new lists or media to outperform what you are now using; sometimes they do, but most of the time they don't.

This estimating exercise should be repeated at least once a year and during the year if conditions change materially. If your company acquires another related company, if a new and well-financed competitor enters the market, or something similar happens, then you will have to immediately re-estimate all your numbers. Checklist 43 should be used as a starting point. Eventually, you should construct a master chart of all your products and their contributions to sales. Detailed estimates should be made, campaign by campaign, allowing for circumstances like a postage increase, for example, in order to accurately forecast costs. As time goes on, you will refine the process so that your forecasts will become remarkably accurate and reliable.

4 Checklists for Space Advertising

MAGAZINES   The primary industry source for information about which magazines reach your target market is *Standard Rate and Data Service* (SRDS). Many larger libraries carry some of their publications. SRDS includes information on various categories of media, including business publications, consumer magazines, farm publications, newspapers, and others. These lists are updated weekly. They contain most of the information you might need, including the following:

Media code

Publisher's editorial profile

Personnel

Commission and cash discount

General rate policy

Black/white rates

Color rates

Covers

Inserts

Bleed

Special position

Contract and copy regulations

Mechanical requirements

Issue and closing dates

Circulation

The purpose of space advertising is to contact the widest number of prospects at a relatively low cost. You may find that several magazines have similar readerships and you may have to choose among them to determine the best one for your product or service.

Analyzing Magazine Circulation   One method of analyzing magazines is to compare their cost per thousand (CPM). CPM is useful when you have magazines with overlapping or similar readership demographics and psychographics, even though they may have different circulations and charge different rates. When you determine CPM, you will have one basis for comparison.

To determine CPM, divide the total cost for the advertising space by the total circulation:

$$\frac{\text{Cost of Ad Space (\$)}}{\text{Total Circulation}} = \text{CPM}$$

For example, a magazine with a cost of $3,500 per page and a circulation of 70,000 would have a CPM of $50:

$$\$3,500 \div 70,000 = \$50 \text{ CPM}$$

An even more effective measure is cost per interested thousand (CPIM). To use CPIM, you need to examine the circulation breakdown. You may discover, to use our hypothetical example, that of the 70,000 circulation, some 50,000 fit into your target market and 20,000 don't.

$$\frac{\text{Cost of Ad Space (\$)}}{\text{Target Market within Circulation}} = \text{CPIM}$$

or

$$\$3,500 \div 50,000 = \$70 \text{ CPIM}$$

Other measures are cost per response (CPR) and cost per order (CPO), neither of which you can determine until after you have used the media. CPR combines the number of inquiries and orders, and CPO measures only orders taken. The mathematics for these two measures is as follows:

$$\frac{\text{Cost of Ad Space (\$)}}{\text{Number of Responses (Including Orders)}} = \text{CPR}$$

or

$$\frac{\text{Cost of Ad Space (\$)}}{\text{Number of Orders}} = \text{CPO}$$

In addition to determining the specific media to use, you need to establish your objectives for each advertisement and a quantifiable goal for each. As a generalization, space is less costly than direct mail or telemarketing on a CPM basis, but its responses can be much lower. Until you have experience to the contrary, avoid setting your monetary space advertising goals at much above the break-even point.

Checklist 48, Setting and Quantifying Space Advertising Objectives, will help you sort out the elements and/or point of view you wish to include in a space ad. If your objective is to sell an item via a space ad, each item that makes it easier for a customer to respond should increase your response rate, however, some of the items will also incur cost. Including an address where orders are to be sent or a coupon to be mailed in the customer's own envelope will add no costs, but you can expect a lower rate of response than offering a toll-free telephone number or an insert card, both of which will add cost.

While it is possible to have more than one objective for a space ad, this checklist should help you focus on which objectives a particular ad is meant to achieve. You may not be able to quantify every item. For example, #4, Retail store support, is difficult to track. It can be a valid objective for an ad, but you can only quantify it by calling the store manager and learning what impact the ad had on store traffic and sales of the items advertised. Even then, the results may be vague.

Once you have set your objectives and determined the quantifiable goal to measure its effectiveness, you may want to put in place a follow-up plan designed to:

1. Convert inquiries to orders.

2. Expand the sale.

3. Verify leads.

Magazine Media Selection

Before you start making decisions about the best magazines in which to advertise your product, you should ask for a copy of each magazine's *Audited Publisher's Statement*. There are several auditing agencies for magazines. Their function is to verify that the circulation claimed by the magazines is accurate. Some of these agencies include the Audit Bureau of Circulations, Business Publications Audit of Circulations, and the Magazine Publishers Association.

MEDIA KITS

Another way of finding out more about a magazine is to request a media kit from the publisher. The media kit generally consists of a folder with the rate card and assorted advertising pieces and/or reprints that support the publisher's claims about the quality of its readership. The *Audited Publisher's Statement* may also be included, but to make sure, ask for this statement when you request a media kit.

RATE CARD

The rate card is the document that gives information on the cost of advertisements for each size and the frequency discounts, if any. It also provides the size specifications for full- or partial-page advertisements, and it gives the dates by which you must send in your reservations and mechanicals to be included in a particular issue. The rate card may also include information about agency commissions, payment terms, and costs for color and special positions.

BINGO CARDS

A bingo card is often called a reader service card by the magazine. It is generally a postage-paid reply card that is easy for readers to fill out and mail in to request more information or a catalog from any advertiser that wishes to participate. It can be a good source for getting many replies or inquiries, but because it is so easy to use, the quality of most leads is usually poor. If you want to impress your management with a high number of responses, the bingo card will most certainly increase the quantity of responses to your ad; if you want qualified leads, do not use the bingo card.

Choosing Among Magazines

In every field, consumer or industrial, you will have magazines that overlap in subscriber bases. You may wish to select only one magazine, or you may decide to go into different magazines that reach similar audiences. The following chart may help you decide whether to advertise in a single magazine or multiple magazines.

Single Magazine Strategy	**Multiple Magazine Strategy**
Advantages:	*Advantages:*
Lower CPM for your target audience	Broader reach of target market
Increased frequency	Target market receives multiple exposure to your ads
Higher frequency discount	
Disadvantage:	*Disadvantages:*
Readerships rarely overlap 100 percent. You may miss part of your target market.	High cost to reach incremental target market
	Depending on budget, may reduce overall frequency
	If frequency is reduced in a magazine, impact on readership of that magazine may be reduced

If there are two magazines whose readership overlaps in your target market, you may need to analyze the differences between them. Following is an example of such an analysis:

	Magazine A	Magazine B	A and B
Circulation	100,000	100,000	
Percentage of target market	80%	80%	100%
Percentage of target market overlap	60%	60%	
Ad cost	$6,000	$7,000	$13,000
CPIM	$60	$70	
Average CPIM			$65

For the purpose of this example, we will assume that the combined readership of both magazines reaches 100 percent of your target market. The lowest cost to reach 80,000 of your target market of 100,000 would be $6,000 (Magazine A), and so your cost to reach the additional 20,000 of your target market would be $7,000. Using our CPIM formula, we would divide 20 into $7,000 for a $350 CPIM (magazine B). One strategy to avoid this high CPIM to reach the remainder of your target market would be to alternate media every so often (e.g., three months in Magazine A followed by three months in Magazine B, and so on).

Checklist 49, Placing Magazine Ads, will help you reserve space in a magazine and provide your copy and art staff or your agency with the information they need to prepare the ad. This checklist serves as a summary of dates and operations, and it prompts you to make some decisions, especially if you are testing an ad. Some larger magazines have regional issues so if your product is not sold nationally, you can save money by choosing editions that are sold within your geographic market only. In addition, some magazines offer A/B splits. This is a technique for testing ads whereby you provide two different ads for the same product and the magazine sends one version to half its customers and the second version to the other half. Ideally, the distribution should be evenly divided across zip codes. Check with the magazine to see how it handles an A/B distribution. If customers are not divided evenly across zip codes the results could be skewed by regional differences.

NEWSPAPERS The primary industry source for information about the cost and circulation of newspapers is Standard Rate and Data Service (SRDS). Larger libraries carry some of their publications. There are separate SRDS publications for community publications, Hispanic media and markets, and newspaper rates and data. These publications contain most of the information you might need including media code, editorial profile, personnel, commission and cash discounts, general rate policy, black and white and color rates, inserts, bleed, special position, contracts, mechanical requirements, issue and closing dates, and circulation (numbers and area).

Checklist 50, Placing Newspaper Ads, will help you ensure that you have covered everything you need to know about reserving the space and preparing the ad. You may create an ad for a number of different newspapers or for a specific paper. Many larger newspapers offer several different sections every day, and it is important that your ad be placed in that section your target audience is likely to read. If specialty sections you want to be in are not run daily, you need to know that so the day of the week could be significant.

If you don't care where or what day your ad will run, you might get a special lower rate for ROP (run of press) where the newspaper will fit your ad in an unsold space. If your ad is to be ROP, the issue date might be changed from a specific day to "the week of," and you would leave blank the day of week, special position and bleed.

A few very large newspapers offer regional editions, which, if your product is not national or your budget is limited, could save you money—you can select one or more regions rather than the whole run.

Magazines Versus Newspapers

Generally, many advertisers use both magazines and newspapers for consumer products. There are differences between them as listed here:

Advantages of Magazine Advertising	**Advantages of Newspaper Advertising**
Longer readership life	Shorter lead times
High per-copy readership	Lower local retail rates
Ads less affected by local or national news	Most readers see paper the same day
High-quality paper stock enhances look of ads	Generally lower cost

If your product is sold in retail stores, newspapers should probably be a part of your promotion strategy. If your product is such that it requires a full-color advertisement to show it effectively, you may be tempted to avoid newspapers, but many products that are normally shown in full color do use black-and-white photography or illustrations in newspapers. Readers do not expect the same quality of illustrations from newspapers as they do from magazines.

FREESTANDING INSERTS

Checklist 51, Placing Freestanding Inserts, deals with those sections, often included with newspapers, that are for advertisers only—there is no editorial matter. Generally, freestanding inserts are in full color and are placed one, two, three, or four to a page. Many freestanding inserts have order forms or coupons for the recipient to cut out and mail. When ordering your space, the publisher will tell you the area in which your coupon must be placed since, on the reverse side of your ad, is another advertiser's ad with its own coupon. Coupons should not be placed so that the coupon on the obverse side is damaged when the recipient cuts out yours. Freestanding inserts are relatively inexpensive and effective, so if your product is intended for the general consumer, it might be worth trying.

12 Checklists
for Catalogs

A catalog is the basic sales tool of most firms that sell products or provide services. There are many different types of catalogs, and they each may have different objectives. However, the most common purpose of a catalog is to provide a list of what the firm has to sell.

Some catalogs are merely price lists of every product or service with no descriptive information. Other catalogs show the product in use in full color. In many cases, more than one type of catalog may be appropriate. For example, a firm may have a simple price list for use by purchasing agents, salespeople, or order takers; an annotated price list for specifiers who need technical data on the product; a catalog with descriptive text and possibly photographs or drawings of the product; and a pictorial approach emphasizing the product in use with minimal descriptive text. Of course, there are variations on these and other combinations of text and illustration.

SETTING CATALOG OBJECTIVES

The first step in preparing a catalog is to set objectives. These objectives often depend on the target market.

In the following example, the purpose and goals for purchasing agents and the sales staff would be satisfied by a price list. For purchasing agents the price list might be more elaborate than for the sales staff, because a subsidiary goal is to give purchasing agents insights into the type of service they can anticipate (24-hour emergency phone number; guaranteed 2-day delivery, etc.). If your target market consists of decision makers, you probably need a strong sales vehicle.

Target Market	Purpose of Catalog	Direct Response Goal
Purchasing agents	Provide prices, discounts, shipping, and other specifications	Convenience, influence sale
Sales staff	Provide prices and discounts	Speed, accuracy
Decision makers	Provide lists of benefits and show product	Recommend or specify purchase

Checklist 52, Setting Catalog Objectives, will help you identify the different target markets and others who use your catalogs. Next, decide what purpose the catalog is to serve for those audiences, as well as your goals for the catalog within those discrete markets.

Once you have decided on your objectives for each catalog, you are ready to determine how to create and budget for each one you will produce. In the previous example, you determined that you needed two different catalogs that contained only price information. However, you might decide that the salespeople's catalog should not be a catalog *per se,* but rather price information that is photocopied and sent to the field on a weekly or monthly basis. You may also decide that because of budgetary constraints you don't want a separate price list type of catalog for pur-chasing agents, but rather you will include price list sheets in the back of your regular catalog or in a special colored-paper section elsewhere within the catalog.

These are your decisions based on marketing objectives, budgetary constraints, and your department's size and ability to schedule and pro-duce several catalogs within specific time periods.

ALLOCATING CATALOG SPACE

If you are creating a new catalog whose purpose is to serve as a primary or secondary sales vehicle, it is important to have a rational basis on which to decide how much space each item in the catalog should have. If the catalog is a price list with limited copy and descriptions of basically the same length, the decision is not a matter of how many descriptive lines a particular product should have, but whether it should have some descrip-tive text or none.

People creating a new catalog often base their size allocations on the sales potential of each item—the greater the potential, the more space is allocated. Another method would be to assign the newest products the most space, on the theory that older products are more familiar to your customers and therefore less description is needed. However, if a product is selling well, giving it a smaller space in the catalog could make customers think that it will be replaced soon with a newer version. After you have determined how much space each item should receive and how many pages your indexes, order forms, and front and back matter will occupy, you can determine the number of pages of your catalog.

Checklist 53, Catalog Page Estimator (A), will help you decide how many pages you need in a catalog. Simply list each item to appear in your catalog and estimate its length. In your first pass, put down the size that you believe the item deserves. Later you will have to make adjustments so that the total number of catalog pages is appropriate for the printing signature size and your total budget. See the example on the following page of how you might complete Checklist 45.

To determine the number of pages, multiply the unit size times the number of units in each column.

For example, four 1/4-page units = $4 \times \frac{1}{4} = 1$ page.

Example of Checklist 53 Catalog Page Estimator (A)

Item	2-Page Spread	1 Page	3/4 Page	1/2 Page	1/3 Page	1/4 Page	1/6 Page	1/8 Page
#807	✓							
#792		✓						
#231		✓						
#844		✓						
#102		✓						
#333		✓						
#690			✓					
#215			✓					
#216				✓				
#357				✓				
#201				✓				
#773					✓			
#202					✓			
#205					✓			
#207							✓	
#198							✓	
#854							✓	
#972							✓	
#960							✓	
#206							✓	
#74							✓	
#12							✓	
Totals:	1	5	2	3	3	0	8	
Total Pages	2	5	1.5	1.5	1	0	1	

Total Pages 12

Checklist 54, Catalog Page Estimator (B) uses a slightly different method to calculate catalog size by the percentage of a page assigned for each item. *Live area* refers to the portion of the page used for text and illustrations. The area surrounding the live area is the *margin*. The *front matter* and *back matter* are pages that do not contain product information. Here's an example of how it works. In the example, the page size is 8-1/2" × 11"; the live area on each page is 7" × 10".

A	**B**	**C**	**D**	**E**
Item Size (100% = 1 Page)	**Square Inches per Unit**	**Number of Units**	**Gross Live Area**[a]	**Number of Pages per Item Size**[b]
100%	70	5	350 sq in	5
50%	35	13	455 sq in	6.5
25%	17.5	33	577.5 sq in	8.25
Sales page totals		51	1,382.5 sq in	19.75 pages
Front matter pages	70	1	70	1
Index pages	70	2	140	2
Back matter pages	70	1	70	1
Order form[c]	70	4	280	(4)
Cover[d]	70	4	280	(4)
Total Pages[e]				24 (rounded up)

[a] Column B × Column C.

[b] Column D ÷ 70 inches (square inches per page)

[c] If the order form is an insert, do not include it in figuring the number of catalog pages.

[d] If the cover is printed on different stock from the interior pages, do not include it in figuring the number of catalog pages.

[e] For this example the order form is an insert and the cover is printed on different paper stock. Therefore, neither is counted in the total number of pages.

There are 50 catalog items (C) taking 20 pages (rounded up) (E), plus 4 pages of other matter for a total of 24 pages, plus cover and order form.

Allocating Catalog Space According to Budgeted Revenue

There are many decisions to be made before making the space allocation for each catalog item. Often, the catalog budget is based on the previous year's activities and results plus this year's new product introductions. If yours is a first-time catalog, the catalog budget will probably be set based on the anticipated relationship between expenses and income. If your catalog sales goal is three times the cost, all the costs must be calculated to determine how much you can spend on printing and preparation. Still another way to determine the space to be allocated to each item in the catalog is to estimate each item's sales and allocate space accordingly.

Obviously, this method is acceptable only for the purpose of setting size relationships. The problem with following it exactly is that in a 24-page catalog with 20 selling pages, Item 1 would take six pages and Item 10, one-twelfth of a page, possibly making Item 1 too large and Item 10 too small. You can use **Checklist 55** to make your own space allocations based on the estimated percentage of budgeted revenue from each item in the catalog.

Item Number	Budgeted Revenue	Percentage of Budgeted Revenue	Number of Pages in Catalog (Rounded Off)
1	$150,000	30%	6
2	125,000	25	5
3	100,000	20	4
4	50,000	10	2
5	30,000	6	1
6	15,000	3	$^1/_2$
7	10,000	2	$^1/_2$
8	10,000	2	$^1/_3$
9	7,000	1.4	$^1/_3$
10	3,000	.6	$^1/_3$
Total	$500,000	100%	

POSTAGE AND MAILING COSTS

Postage Costs

Checklist 56, Estimating Catalog Postage Costs, asks you to examine the two primary determinants of postage costs: weight and thickness. Catalog weight is determined by the trim size, paper stock weight, cover stock weight, and number of pages plus inserts.

Generally catalogs of 32 pages or more will weigh more than the maximum 3.3067 oz. that the post office allows for using the third-class bulk mail rate. In addition, the post office also disallows a mailing piece of more than $^1/_4$-inch thickness to use that rate. Items larger than $^1/_4$-inch thick or weighing more than 3.3067 oz. (but less than one pound) qualify for the third-class pound rate. Check with your local postmaster for the current rates.

There are many opportunities to qualify for postal discounts based on the type of center to which your bulk mailing is delivered as well as the presort or label bar coding used. If you are not familiar with bulk rate discounts, visit your local postmaster and get the details as well as Form 3602-R.

Note: the cost of a bulk rate permit is not included on Checklist 56 since its cost should be prorated over all the catalogs you mail in a year, thereby making its impact on the unit mailing cost negligible.

Mailing Costs

Use **Checklist 57,** Estimating Catalog Mailing Costs, alongside Checklist 56. It will help you estimate your costs per piece. Divide one pound by the weight of an individual catalog to determine the number of catalogs per pound, then divide the number of catalogs per pound into the pound rate and add the per piece rate to determine the unit postage cost. Next add the mailing list rates, merge/purge costs, and the lettershop costs to get your total mailing cost.

Merge/purge involves taking the entire mailing list in electronic form, and combining all the lists into a single list in strict zip code order. Giving your lettershop a zip sequence tape will reduce sorting costs, but more important, the merge/purge program will identify the majority of duplicate addresses and automatically purge excess names. If on a mailing of 100,000 catalogs, there is a 5% duplication, you will mail 5,000 fewer catalogs. If each catalog cost 30 cents to mail and 50 cents to produce, you would save 80 cents each or $4,000 plus another few hundred dollars on reduced sorting costs. Since you paid for the 5,000 names that were eliminated, you can still use them for a future mailing. Because these names are on more than one mailing list, they are probably excellent prospects.

CATALOG PRODUCTION SCHEDULE

Checklist 58, Catalog Production Schedule, provides a worksheet to keep track of the due dates for the elements of a catalog. You will note that there are two separate columns for price checking—one at the beginning when the copy is submitted and one at the end before going to press. We use the term "drop dead date" to mean the date after which no additions or deletions should be made. As a catalog goes through the process of creation, changes get more expensive with each step. If you are responsible for the catalog budget and someone wants to make a significant change after the drop-dead date, it will materially impact your costs.

If yours is a full color catalog, you should probably budget the cost of the designer, production manager, and/or yourself to be at the printing plant for a final color check before the press run begins.

Planning Catalog Revisions

Checklist 59, Planning Catalog Revisions, is based on reviewing several factors. After you have analyzed the sales results of each item in the catalog, you will want to make the appropriate size adjustments as discussed earlier. You will want to add new items and delete products that are no longer in inventory. You will probably want a new cover. You may even decide to have a whole new design or to keep the old design and merely change prices. This checklist serves as a reminder of the kind of revisions you may wish to make for the next edition of a catalog.

The Catalog Budget
When preparing the catalog budget, it is important to include every operation that will be charged to the catalog. Indirect expenses, such as salaries, might not be included in the costs, whereas services you must hire outside probably would be. The decision to include staff salaries in the costs of a catalog may depend on the amount of time a particular person spends working on the catalog. In some cases, if catalogs are a major portion of a department's activities, the cost of the catalog traffic, production, copy, and art staffs may be prorated among the various catalogs, but the salaries of others who play more minor roles in catalog production may not be included.

Staff Salaries
Checklist 60, Time Allocation for In-House Staff on Catalogs, is for allocating a portion of the salaries of catalog production people among the various catalogs your department produces. In this example we use six catalogs. (These are purely hypothetical numbers.)

Catalogs

Staff Person or Group	1	2	3	4	5	6	Total
Art director	15%	5%	10%	5%	5%	20%	60%
Illustrator	15%	5%	15%	5%	15%	55%	100%
Photographer	10%	5%	10%	5%	5%	15%	50%
Production manager	10%	10%	10%	10%	10%	20%	70%
Copy chief	10%	5%	10%	5%	10%	20%	60%
Copywriters	10%	5%	10%	5%	10%	20%	60%
Traffic	10%	15%	20%	15%	15%	25%	100%
Typesetter	20%	5%	20%	5%	10%	40%	100%

Taking the total cost of the catalog, determine the expense allocated to each item for sale in the catalog. The front matter, back matter, and inserts do not directly account for any sales. They are part of catalog overhead, and their cost must be borne by the items for sale. For example, for a 24-page catalog, of which four pages are reserved for front matter and back matter, the analysis is on the basis of 20 pages.

In the following example, the catalog (24 pages plus cover and insert) costs $144,000. The sales goal is to bring in $3 of revenue for every $1 spent on the catalog. Each item is scrutinized as to whether it pulled its share of anticipated sales.

Cost per Allocated Space (based on 20 sales pages)

Allocated Space (Pages)	Allocation Method	Allocated Cost
Two-page spread	2 pages is 1/10 of catalog sales pages	$14,000
One page	1 page is 1/20 of catalog sales pages	7,200
One-half page	1/2 page is 1/40 of catalog sales pages	3,600
One-quarter page	1/4 page is 1/80 of catalog sales pages	1,800
One-sixth page	1/6 page is 1/144 of catalog sales pages	1,000
One-eighth page	1/8 page is 1/160 of catalog sales pages	900
Allocated Size (%)		
1%	Each 1% is 1/100 of a page	$72.00 per 1%

The following example shows how to analyze the results from our catalog mailing:

Item	Page Size	Allocated Cost	Expected Revenue	Actual Revenue	Space Allocation Decision
1	Full	$7,200	$21,600	$24,000	Maintain size
2	1/2	3,600	10,800	4,300	Reduce to 1/4 page
3	1/4	1,800	5,400	5,000	Maintain size (?)
4	1/4	1,800	5,400	10,000	Increase to 1/2 page
	Percentage of one page				
5	33%	2,376	7,128	15,000	Increase to 50%
6	20%	1,440	4,320	5,100	Maintain size

Checklist 61, Catalog Production Estimator, attempts to cover all the aspects of catalog production up to and including ordering the lists, mailing, and shipping the remaining catalogs to your warehouse or other facilities. The column, headed *Cost estimate* can be your own budgeted figures or the actual bids from suppliers. It is critical to fill in the actual cost next to each item and to understand what accounted for the differences. This checklist will help you budget for future catalogs and anticipate areas where you have had problems in the past.

You can use **Checklists 62 and 63** to estimate the appropriate size of items in your catalog: Checklist 50 by increments of page size; Checklist 51 by percentage increments.

10 Checklists for Card Packs and Package Inserts

CARD PACKS A card pack consists of a number of individual business reply cards bundled together in some sort of mailing envelope or package and sent to a selected mailing list. Sometimes the cards are from one advertiser, with each card devoted to a separate product; at other times a number of advertisers share the same mailing vehicle, each competing for attention much as they do in other print media.

Card packs started as an incentive to advertisers in business magazines. If an advertiser took a full page in a publication, the advertisement was reproduced in a reduced form on a business reply card and mailed to the subscriber list a short time before the issue was published. It was intended to prompt readers to "look for our ad" in the magazine.

Soon advertisers discovered that the 3" × 5" card was an effective sales medium that could generate orders or inquiries at much less cost than a similar investment in magazine space. It was particularly effective for book publishers, which could use a separate card for each book promoted. Today there are hundreds of card packs going to audiences ranging from accountants to woodworking prospects.

Using card packs effectively involves three important steps:

1. Research existing card packs and select the right one for your product.

2. Create an effective card using copy and visual appeals.

3. Track results so effective cards can be repeated and ineffective ones eliminated from the schedule.

Researching Existing Card Packs The first step in researching card decks is to consult *Card Deck Rates and Data,* published semi-annually by Standard Rate and Data Service, 3004 Glenview Road, Wilmette, IL 60091. It includes information on more than 700 business and consumer card decks and is available from the publisher directly, at larger libraries, or from your advertising agency.

Choosing a card pack is much like choosing a mailing list: the first question to ask is whether the mailing list used by the card deck publisher goes to the audience you seek. The same standards are applied to the list as in a direct mail campaign. A list of mail-order buyers is usually more productive than a subscriber list, and a subscriber list is more productive than a prospect list generated from a variety of sources.

The information in SRDS is brief regarding the source of the lists used by the various card deck publishers. Once you have a number of card decks for which you want additional information, contact the card deck publisher or manager directly and ask for a media kit. The media kit usually will include a sample of the deck so you can see what kind of advertisers are using the deck, plus more extensive information on the source of the list used, the demographics of the audience, and other details.

To select an appropriate card pack, first summarize the important facts on **Checklist 64,** Card Pack Audience Ranking. Cost per thousand (CPM) is an effective measure of how much it costs to reach a prospect. Once you have completed the checklist, you will be in a better position to judge which card decks will be most productive. Rank them in order of value for your sales effort and test the highest-ranking card decks first. If those work, you can repeat them in a later mailing and add lower-ranking decks until you reach those that are not productive.

Once you have some experience in using card decks, you will have to budget for them on an annual basis. **Checklist 65,** Card Pack Planner, will help you budget mailing quantities and advertising dollars for each month and for the whole year.

Creating an Effective Card

The card in a pack has been aptly called a "one-second billboard." Studies have shown that the average recipient of a deck will open the pack over a wastebasket, flip through all the cards quickly, and discard most of them immediately. This is in contrast to a catalog or a direct-mail piece that may be looked at briefly when received and then referred to later. Therefore, you have a fleeting second in which to make an impression on the prospect.

Card packs should be treated as seriously as any other part of your media plan. This means using your best copywriters and artists to create the cards and making the finished art match the printing process. Since cards are usually printed on a web press using rather absorbent card stock, you should avoid fine printing screens or unusually small type. **Checklist 66,** Card Pack Effectiveness, reviews these and other details you should be aware of.

The first, foremost, and oldest rule of copy is to promise a benefit up front, usually in the headline. Amplify it in a subhead or two, expand on them in the copy, and you have your basic card copy. Do not try to include all the material you put in a direct mail campaign—there is simply no room. Rather, hit your reader with a big benefit and follow up with one or two "proof" statements.

If you are selling something very expensive and you have an inquiry handling system (see Checklist 69), you may want the copy to solicit inquiries rather than an outright sale. There is no hard-and-fast rule regarding a cost barrier that defines when you should ask for an order or an inquiry. Some book publishers routinely solicit direct sales of products costing more than $100 using only the card pack format. However, manufacturers of major industrial equipment costing hundreds of thousands of dollars would solicit inquiries, not direct sales.

Make sure you leave plenty of room for the prospect to write a legible name and address. This is also the place for a guarantee of satisfaction and any other information you require from the customer or prospect. Avoid using credit card information on an open-face card. It is unlawful to send it without the security of a sealed envelope, and most prospects would be unlikely to bother finding an envelope and a stamp to respond. Better to offer to send it out with an invoice. In this case, you would need to set up procedures to monitor the bad debts generated. A reasonable proportion of bad debts to invoices paid promptly can be tolerated as a cost of doing business.

Checklist 67, Card Deck Copy/Art Requisition, will make it easy for you to organize the creative work of producing cards for various mailings. Usually, it is best to keep the original art in your own files and send a reproduction or film to the card deck printer. This way, you will always have a master copy of the advertisement that can be revised or updated with new key numbers.

Checklist 68, Card Deck Insertion Order, is a standardized way to handle all the details of insertion. It is important that keys be accurately specified and double-checked on mailing samples, because this will influence your future decisions about whether to repeat the card. On Checklist 68, there are four spaces for keys to take care of possible split-run tests. If you plan on testing four different prices of a product in the October 1994 issue of *Working Artist,* you might pick keys as follows:

Price A	WA1094A
Price B	WA1094B
Price C	WA1094C
Price D	WA1094D

Tracking Results   It is important to track all orders or inquiries by individual card deck and mailing date. **Checklist 69,** Card Pack Order/Inquiry Record, will help you do this with minimum trouble.

Use a separate form for each card deck and product being promoted. A looseleaf notebook is probably the best way to handle this chore, unless you enter the results directly in a computer database. The cost is the cost of the card deck less any discounts you earn for frequency. Your dollar goal or number of inquiries is what you determine you need to break even or produce a required profit.

When you get the first order or inquiry, enter that in week 1, and fill in succeeding weeks with results as they come in. By the fifth week, you will usually see the orders trailing off a great deal, and you can enter all remaining orders in that week. Track the returns in the appropriate column and, finally, calculate your net orders or inquiries in the last column.

Compare this with Column 4—your goal—and you will readily see whether this mailing has been profitable.

As you repeat the exposure in future mailings, you will be able to compare results for the same product in the same deck at different times of the year. You may discover seasonal trends, the effects of competition, or a change in the composition of the list being used. You can also test different versions of the offer and see which ones work best.

PACKAGE INSERTS

If you've ever ordered a product by mail, you probably found in the bottom of the shipping box several brochures for other products you might be interested in ordering. They are often the same company's brochures; it is an attempt to increase the company's business without additional mailing expense.

In other cases the box will contain an envelope with a number of brochures from several different companies. These brochures constitute a package insert program on the part of the original mailer. The company is mailing you a product, so it makes sense to include brochures from other, noncompeting companies that might want to solicit your interest in other products. The original mailer can estimate how many packages it ships in a specific period and sell "circulation," much as a magazine sells space in its pages.

Package inserts should be considered in two lights:

1. If your company is mailing several thousand packages a month to a specialized audience of mail-order buyers, you have the makings of a successful package insert program. You might want to explore your potential for profit with a list broker.

2. If your company is looking for additional exposure for its products, you should look into a package insert program. Details of what is available and who you can reach using such programs is available from a list broker or from the previously mentioned Standard Rate and Data Service.

Unlike card decks, package inserts allow you leeway in format. Some mailers will permit a fairly large piece, like a double-folded page. Others might limit you to a single piece resembling an oversized postcard. The specs vary widely; request media cards and rates from the mailer or a list broker that will tell you everything you need to create the piece. You can often use an existing advertising piece if you can add a key code that will identify that it was used in a particular package insert program.

Use **Checklist 70,** Package Insert Profitability Analysis, to help determine whether to begin a package insert program. Use **Checklist 71,** Insert Program Analysis, to help determine what characteristics to compare its usefulness against other media.

Use **Checklist 72,** Insert Schedule, to keep track of key codes and quantities mailed. Because you have no control over the mail schedule—it all depends on how many packages the mailer sends each month—you must be patient for results. They will sometimes dribble in month after month, and you should be prepared to maintain the records for months before evaluating the results.

Checklist 73, Insert Results Analysis, will tell you whether a program is working and whether it should be repeated or expanded. The goals are the same as for card decks; quantities and CPM numbers give you some comparison figures among different programs. If results keep coming in beyond Week 5, you man want to expand the form horizontally or put it on a computer spreadsheet.

Card decks and package insert programs are important adjuncts to a marketing campaign consisting of direct mail pieces, catalogs, and space advertising. You may find, as other advertisers have discovered, that these two programs offer the most profit for the dollars spent.

7 Checklists for Telemarketing

Telemarketing can be used effectively for direct sales, research, sales support, publicity, and a host of other purposes. Telemarketing can work as a solo campaign or as a follow-up to a direct response campaign. Moreover, telemarketing can be outbound or inbound. In outbound telemarketing, telemarketers call prospects; in inbound telemarketing, prospects call telemarketers, usually as a result of a space ad or direct mail contact.

Telemarketing, both inbound and outbound, in conjunction with direct mail can have a dramatic effect on results. If, for example, a direct mail piece generated a 1 percent response, offering customers the convenience of a toll-free ordering number might lift that response by 0.5 percent. If an outbound telemarketing campaign were directed at the recipients of the direct mail campaign, the total order response could be increased up to 10 percent or more.

ADVANTAGES OF TELEMARKETING

1. Shorter lead time required to set up a telemarketing test than a direct mail test

2. Relatively short time to determine whether campaign is working

3. Ability of marketing managers to closely monitor test and roll-out

4. Ease of changes in script, offer, or other campaign elements

5. Ease of modifying or expanding size of campaign depending on initial results

6. Personalization of customer contact

7. Ease of upselling according to individual customer response. (In upselling, the telemarketer attempts to sell the prospect allied products and/or services after the initial sale or in lieu of it if there has been no sale.)

DISADVANTAGES OF TELEMARKETING

1. Fewer customer contacts (Depending on the message length, a completed call may take 3–10 minutes, or 6 to 20 people contacted per hour.)

2. Restricted number of hours operators can sound fresh (Six hours is maximum for an operator in a day; the rest of the day is spent on paperwork.)

3. Higher cost per contact than direct mail.

4. Telemarketer training required for each product or service sold (Unless there is a script with little customer interaction, operators should have training on each product plus a good, easy-to-use product guide.)

5. Frustration of locating the right prospects for your product or service (Telemarketers often struggle to get past the secretary only to learn that the product has no relevance to the prospect.)

6. Frustration of not finding the right prospects in (Telemarketers often play "telephone tag," but the prospect rarely calls back.)

7. Calls to the opposite coast require double shifts (National telemarketers must accommodate a three-hour time difference.)

8. Ensuring that operator abilities meet customer expectations (Avoid having an operator read a script to a busy manager. This is a sure turn-off and hang-up.)

THE CHECKLISTS

In this section, you will find checklists and forms that should be helpful for running a telemarketing campaign. Telemarketing can be challenging and rewarding. There is no magic; it requires planning, training, experience, careful execution, and common sense.

Checklist 74, Account Analysis, lists the key contacts at each company your telemarketers call on. It should be updated as frequently as possible since business personnel continually changes. The contacts are listed in order of importance.

Checklist 75, Competition Analysis, is a convenient way of capturing information about key competitors. As your telemarketers talk to their customers and prospects, they should be attentive to any comments that may be made about your competitors—positive or negative. Some customers may be uncomfortable talking about your competitors, others will enjoy doing so. It is often not a good idea to denigrate your competition unless the customer has brought up the subject or is asking your telemarketer about something a competitor has said about your company. The market share column refers to the impression the telemarketer gets about competitors from talking to their customers. The marketing method column might indicate: telemarketing (tm); direct mail (dm); retail (r); sales force (sf); or any other significant operation or channel.

Checklist 76, Audience Analysis, is information a telemarketer can use as background information so that he or she can understand your target market better. This is especially useful when you are using an outside telemarketing agency.

Checklist 77, Campaign Set-up, contains the kind of questions telemarketers will be asking about the campaign. You should have the answers to each of the questions before you start the telemarketing campaign.

Checklist 78, Inbound Telemarketing Project Checklist, is extremely detailed, and it covers all the aspects needed to set up an inbound telemarketing project. You should review this with the telemarketing manager to make sure that there are no surprises during the campaign.

Checklist 79, Outbound Telemarketing Project Checklist, includes every aspect needed to set up and run an outbound telemarketing project. You should review each item with the telemarketing manager, reviewing all their procedures, reports, training, programming, and other aspects important to the success of the project.

Checklist 80, Telemarketing Contact Record, is the report on the result of each customer contact. The follow-up section should be prepared in advance so that the telemarketing representative can select an appropriate package to send to the customer who needs additional information or prodding to make the sale.

Key Media Questions	Description	Yes/No	Comments
Does it reach your target market?	The publication, mailing list, or other media should target the audience you want to reach. Media titles may not tell the whole story. Check the circulation breakdowns carefully.		
Will it generate direct response?	The most responsive direct response media are those generated by direct response. Is the magazine distributed free (controlled circulation), or is it sold by mail or telephone (paid circulation)?		
Does your competition use it?	Is your biggest competitor using this media? If so, that competitor has done some valuable media research at no cost to you. Copy another's success by testing the same media for your offer.		
Is it up-to-date and accurate?	If you're investigating a mailing list, you want the most current names at current addresses. A magazine or journal should reach the people they have identified in the numbers promised. Check professional readership audits for magazines and ask broadcast stations to pinpoint their markets on a map.		

CHECKLIST 31　Media Comparison Chart

Medium	Circulation Reach	Primary Audience (50% or More of Circulation)		Secondary Audience (30% or More of Circulation)		Other (Less than 20% of Circulation)	
	(000s)	%	#	%	#	%	#
1.							
2.							
3.							
4.							
5.							
6.							
7.							
8.							
9.							
10.							
11.							
12.							
13.							
14.							
15.							
16.							
17.							
18.							
19.							
20.							

CHECKLIST 32   Media Ranking Chart

Medium	Rank	Cost per Thousand (CPM)	Size of Ad	Cost per Ad

CHECKLIST 33 Media Calendar

Media	Jan	Feb	Mar	Apr	May	Jun	Jul	Aug	Sep	Oct	Nov	Dec
Direct mail (Number of pieces)												
Campaign A												
Campaign B												
Campaign C												
Telemarketing (List size)												
Campaign A												
Campaign B												
Campaign C												
Space Ads (Circulation)												
Publication A												
Publication B												
Publication C												
Alternative Media												
Campaign A												
Campaign B												
Campaign C												
Radio												
Television												
Infomercial												
Spot TV												
900 number												
Yellow Pages												
Other												

CHECKLIST 34 Lead Generation by Sales Representative

Medium: _____ Date/Issue: _____

Production Cost: _____ Media Cost: _____ Total Cost: _____

Lead Source: **C** (Coupon); **IS** (Insert card with stamp); **IN** (Insert card, no stamp) **W** (Write-in); **T** (Toll-free call)

Representative	Issue Date	Lead Source	Date	Date	Date	Date	Date
1.							
2.							
3.							
4.							
5.							
6.							
7.							
8.							
9.							
10.							
11.							
12.							
13.							
14.							
15.							
16.							
17.							
18.							
19.							
20.							
21.							
22.							
23.							
24.							
25.							
26.							
27.							
28.							
29.							
30.							

CHECKLIST 35 Tracking Leads

Representative	Goal	Week 1	Week 2	Week 3	Week 4	Week 5	Sales Resulting Directly from Leads

CHECKLIST 36   Estimating Media Reach to Generate Leads

1	2	3	4	5	6	7
Representative	Number of Leads Required Monthly[a]	Media	Circulation (000s)	Average Percentage of Inquiry Response[b]	Average Percentage of Qualified Leads[c]	Actual Number of Qualified Leads[d]

[a]Multiply leads per day required by number of working days per month for each representative.

[b]The anticipated percentage of response to your ad from the entire circulation.

[c]The anticipated percentage of responses from Column 5 that will result in qualified leads.

[d]Column 4 × Column 5 × Column 6 should approximate Column 7. (Use the actual number of leads for Column 7.)

CHECKLIST 37 Selecting Mailing Lists

Product / Campaign: _____ Date: _____

Mailing Description: _____ **Mail Date:** _____

List Name	Source	Quantity Available	Quantity Ordered	Test / Extension

List Media: ☐ Labels; ☐ Disk (Format: _____); ☐ Tape (Format: _____)

CHECKLIST 38 Sources of Names per Segment

Name of Segment:[a]

1 Sub-segment[b]	2 Format[c]	3 Available From[d]	4 CPM[e]	5 Quantity[f]	6 Total[g]
1.					
2.					
3.					
4.					
5.					
6.					
7.					
8.					

[a]Each major segment should have its own checklist.
[b]For each major segment, indicate the name of all identifiable sub-segments.
[c]Format on which list is available: magnetic tape, labels, directory, or other (specify).
[d]Name of agency that owns the list; permission to use the list will probably be required.
[e]Cost per thousand names, if applicable.
[f]Total number of names in sub-segment.
[g]Total price of one-time rental of sub-segment.

CHECKLIST 39   List Rental Form

List Name	List Source	Date Ordered	Quantity Ordered	Format	Needed By	Delivery Date
1.						
2.						
3.						
4.						
5.						
6.						
7.						
8.						
9.						
10.						

CHECKLIST 40 List Performance Analysis

List Name	Quantity Mailed	Quantity Remaining	Response Goal (# or $)	Actual Responses (# or $)	Selling Cost (%)	Decision
1.						
2.						
3.						
4.						
5.						
6.						
7.						
8.						
9.						
10.						

CHECKLIST 41   Components of a Direct Response Campaign

To: Creative Director or Copy Chief _____

From: _____

Component	✔	Description	Copy Due	Art Due	Mechanical Due
Letter					
Circular					
Envelope					
BRC or BRE					
Lift letter					
Premium flyer					
Other					

Mail Date: _____

☐ First-class   ☐ Bulk mail

Deliver printed materials to: _____

Due Date: _____

Postage check needed by: _____

CHECKLIST 42   Campaign Schedule

Function	Date Assigned	Date Due	Date Approved	Date Delivered
Creative				
Copy				
Other copy (legal approvals)				
Art				
Other art (model releases, etc.)				
Production				
Type				
Photos/illustrations				
Mechanicals				
Other				
Lists				
In-house				
Rental				
Computer services (merge/purge, de-dupe)				
Delivery to lettershop				
Other				
Printing				
Order paper stock				
Mechanical to printer				
Proofs				
Delivery of finished job				
Lettershop				
Postage and permits				
Mail date				

CHECKLIST 43 Analyzing the Direct Mail Campaign

	1 List Name	2 List Quantity	3 Quantity Mailed	4 Quantity Remaining	5 Selling Cost[a]	6 Number of Orders	7 Revenue[b]	8 Cost per Order[c]	9 Selling Cost[d] (%)	10 Decision[e]
1.										
2.										
3.										
4.										
5.										
6.										
7.										
8.										
9.										
10.										

[a]Cost per thousand (CPM) mailed, multiplied by each test list size (e.g., if List A is a total of 25,000 names and the CPM is $400, the selling cost of List A would be 25 × $400, or $10,000.

[b]Income from each list.

[c]Column 5 divided by Column 6.

[d]Column 5 divided by Column 7.

[e]**Retest** (test the same quantity again); **Extend** (test a larger quantity); **Balance** (mail an even larger quantity); **Roll out** (mail to all other names on the list).

Growth Areas	Current Year	Short-Range Goals	Mid-Range Goals	Long-Range Goals
Product line				
Outside mailing lists				
Media (Specify by type; include number of prospects reached)				
Telemarketing				
New technologies (Infomercials, interactive TV, electronic kiosks, 900 numbers)				
Gross margins (Can you cut costs or raise prices to boost margins?)				
In-house customer lists				
Sales				
Marketing expenses				
Staff additions/deletions				
Overhead				
Profits				

CHECKLIST 45   Tracking the Competition

Competitor	Indicate Date					Comments
	Direct Mail	Telemarketing	Space Ads	Trade Shows	Other	

Checklist 46 Mailing List Broker Data

Name: _____

Address: _____

City/State/Zip: _____

Phone: _____ Fax: _____

Account executive: _____

Key clients: _____

_____

Recommendations: _____

_____

Estimate of annual volume of names: _____

Exclusive list manager for: _____

_____

_____

Member of direct response associations: _____

_____

Comments: _____

_____

_____

_____

CHECKLIST 47 Price Analysis

Product _____   Date _____

A	B	C	D					E	F
			Key Competitors' Prices						
Your Test Price	**Estimated Sales**	**Gross Margin**	**Name/ Price**	**Name/ Price**	**Name/ Price**	**Name/ Price**	**Name/ Price**	**Key Competitor**	**Your Minimum Gross Margin**

Column A: Insert a different test price on each line

Column B: Sales should vary with price

Column C: Gross margin may vary as price varies. If a gross margin falls below your company's acceptable gross margin minimum, circle it. There are situations where a low gross margin may be acceptable. Is this one of them?

Column D: List competitors and their prices—except for your key competitor.

Column E: List your key competitor's price here. If the price you select is significantly different from this competitor's, you should have good reasons for using it.

Column F: Indicate your company's minimally acceptable gross margin as a reminder.

CHECKLIST 48   Setting and Quantifying Space Advertising Objectives

Products _____   Magazine _____

Ad Size _____ Issue _____   Circulation _____

Objective	Goal (Quantity)
1. To sell a particular item by including:	
a. An address where orders are to be sent	
b. A coupon to be mailed in the buyer's own envelope	
c. A toll-free telephone number	
d. An insert card or envelope	
2. To gather names for:	
a. A direct mail campaign	
b. Building a mailing list	
c. Catalog mailings	
3. To test a target market for:	
a. Interest in buying the product	
b. Willingness to purchase through the mail	
c. Appropriateness of list	
4. Retail store support	
5. Reinforcement of:	
a. Product benefits	
b. Company image	
6. Market research	
7. Lead gathering for:	
a. Sales force	
b. Telemarketing effort	
Total	

CHECKLIST 49   Placing Magazine Ads

Person Ordering Ad: _____   Phone: _____

Copy Platform: _____

_____

Target Audience: _____

Action Desired: _____

Item	Information Needed	✔
Product		
Magazine		
Issue date		
Special position		
Size of ad		
Number of colors		
Bleed(s)		
Film		
National or regional edition		
A/B split		
Reservation date		
Materials date		
Reply device		
Copy due		
Art due		
Photography due		

CHECKLIST 50   Placing Newspaper Ads

Person Ordering Ad: _____ Phone: _____

Copy Platform: _____

_____

Target Audience: _____

Action Desired: _____

Item	Information Needed	✔
Product		
Newspaper		
Issue date		
Day of week		
Section or ROP		
Special position		
Regional edition(s)		
Size of ad		
Number of colors		
Bleed(s)		
Film		
Reservation date		
Materials date		
Copy due		
Art due		
Photography due		

CHECKLIST 51 Placing Freestanding Inserts

Person Ordering Ad: _____ Phone: _____

Copy Platform: _____

_____

Target Audience: _____

Action Desired: _____

Item	Information Needed	✔
Product		
Newspaper(s)		
Stand-alone		
Issue date		
Coupon placement		
Special position		
Size of ad		
Full color		
Bleed(s)		
Film		
Reservation date		
Materials date		
Copy due		
Art due		
Photography due		

Target Market	Purpose of Catalog	Direct Response Goal

Item	2-Page Spread	1 Page	3/4 Page	1/2 Page	1/3 Page	1/4 Page	1/6 Page	1/8 Page	Other
1.									
2.									
3.									
4.									
5.									
6.									
7.									
8.									
9.									
10.									
11.									
12.									
13.									
14.									
15.									
16.									
17.									
18.									
19.									
20.									
Totals:										Grand Total Pages:
Total Pages:									

A	B	C	D	E
Item Size (100% = 1 Page)	Square Inches per unit	Number of Units	Gross Live Area	Number of Pages per Item Size
200%				
100%				
75%				
50%				
33.3%				
25%				
12.5%				
10%				
Other				
Sales Page Totals				
Front Matter Pages				
Index Pages				
Back Matter Pages				
Order Form				
Cover				
Total # of Pages				

Column D = Column B × Column C.

Column E = Column D ÷ the numer of square inches per page.

CHECKLIST 55 Allocating Catalog Space According to Budgeted Revenue

Item Number	Budgeted Revenue	Percentage of Budgeted Revenue	Number of Pages in Catalog (rounded off)
1.			
2.			
3.			
4.			
5.			
6.			
7.			
8.			
9.			
10.			
11.			
12.			
13.			
14.			
15.			
16.			
17.			
18.			
Total			

CHECKLIST 56 Estimating Catalog Postage Costs

A	B	C	D	E	F	G
Catalog Name	Weight Each*	Discounted Pound Rate	Discounted Piece Rate	Postage Each	Number of Pieces	Postage Total

*If the catalog weighs more than 3.3067 oz. or is more than 1/4-inch thick, it does not qualify for the third-class bulk rate, but must use another classification of mail, probably third-class pound rate.

Column E = Column C + Column D.

Column G = Column E × Column F.

Catalog Name	Postage Total	Mailing Lists	Merge/ Purge	Affixing Labels	Sort/ tie/bag	Total Mailing Cost
Totals						

CHECKLIST 58 Catalog Production Schedule

Catalog Name	Copy Due	Prices Checked	Art Due	Photos Due	Illustrations Due	Cover Art Due	Drop Dead Date*	Film Due	Film to Printer	Inserts Due	Lists Ordered	Press Proofs Due	Final Price Check	Mail Date

*No changes to be made after this date.

CHECKLIST 59 Planning Catalog Revisions

Catalog: _____ Due date: _____

Revisions Needed	Yes	No	Person Responsible	Date Due
Copy				
Design—text				
Design—cover				
Type				
Illustrations/photographs				
Insert/order form				
Paper stock				
Mailing lists/broker				
Lettershop				
Scanner				
Printer				
Other				

125

Staff Person or Group	Catalog						Total
	1	2	3	4	5	6	
Art director							
Assistant art director							
Art technician							
Illustrator (1)							
Illustrator (2)							
Photographer							
Production manager							
Production assistant							
Copy chief							
Copywriter (1)							
Copywriter (2)							
Traffic							
Typesetter (1)							
Typesetter (2)							
Other							

CHECKLIST 61 Catalog Production Cost Estimator

Operation	Cost Estimate	Actual Cost
Copy:		
Writing		
Revisions/changes		
Art:		
Design		
Type		
Type AAs		
Paste-up		
Illustrations		
Photography		
Printing/Paper:		
Separations		
Cover printing/binding		
Cover stock		
Text printing/binding		
Text stock		
Inserts		
Shipping:		
Freight to warehouse		
Mailing:		
Mailing lists/labels		
Sort, tie, bag, mail		
Postage		
Reply card postage		
Totals:		

Total Catalog Cost Estimator: Total direct expenses: $ _____

Total indirect expenses: $ _____

Total cost: $ _____

Item	Size	Allocated Cost	Budgeted Revenue	Actual Revenue	Comment
1.					
2.					
3.					
4.					
5.					
6.					
7.					
8.					
9.					
10.					
11.					
12.					
13.					
14.					
15.					
16.					
17.					
18.					
19.					
20.					
Totals:					

CHECKLIST 63   Catalog Allocation Analyzer by Percentage of a Page

Item	Percentage of One Page	Allocated Cost	Budgeted Revenue	Actual Revenue	Comments
1.					
2.					
3.					
4.					
5.					
6.					
7.					
8.					
9.					
10.					
11.					
12.					
13.					
14.					
15.					
16.					
17.					
18.					
19.					
20.					
Totals:					

CHECKLIST 64 Card Pack Audience Ranking

Card Pack	Circulation	Total Cost	CPM	Frequency	Lists Used	Ranking

CHECKLIST 65 Card Pack Annual Media Planner

	Jan	Feb	Mar	Apr	May	Jun	Jul	Aug	Sep	Oct	Nov	Dec	Totals
Name													
Quantity													
Cost													
Name													
Quantity													
Cost													
Name													
Quantity													
Cost													
Name													
Quantity													
Cost													
Name													
Quantity													
Cost													
Name													
Quantity													
Cost													
Name													
Quantity													
Cost													

CHECKLIST 66   Card Pack Effectiveness

Offer: _____   Card pack: _____   Issue date: _____

Item	✔	Comments
Copy		
Main benefit up front		
Selling points clear in descriptive copy		
Bullets for emphasis		
Length of copy suitable for space		
Special features or offer highlighted		
Clear ordering instructions		
Corner card space utilized		
Key codes included		
Design and Art		
Headlines and subheads distinct		
Readable type (no smaller than 7 point)		
Illustrations/photographs clear (110 screen preferred)		
Color used effectively		
Ample space for customer name and address		
Other		

CHECKLIST 67   Card Deck Copy/Art Requisition

To: Creative Director / Copy Chief ☐ **From:** _____ **Date:** _____

Please prepare a card(s) for the following products:

1. _____

2. _____

3. _____

4. _____

Card Deck Name: _____

Trim Size: _____ Color(s): _____

Format: ☐ Vertical; ☐ Horizontal; ☐ Single; ☐ Double; ☐ Triple

☐ Film; ☐ Mechanical

Copy Due Date: _____

Art Due Date: _____

Date Film/Mechanical Due at Printer: _____

Business Reply Side: ☐ Indicia; ☐ Place for stamp

Special Instructions: _____

_____

_____

_____

_____

_____

CHECKLIST 68 Card Deck Insertion Order

To: _____

_____

_____

_____

From: _____

_____

_____

Card 1 Key No.: _____

Card 2 Key No.: _____

Card 3 Key No.: _____

Card 4 Key No.: _____

Please run the above cards in:

Name of Deck: _____

Issue Date: _____

Specs: No. of Colors:_____: Color Choices:_____

☐ Vertical; ☐ Horizontal; ☐ Single; ☐ Double; ☐ Triple

Art: ☐ Herewith; ☐ To Come

☐ Pick Up From: _____

Purchase Order No.: _____

Date: _____

Phone: _____

Fax: _____

Price: $_____

Run: ☐ Full; ☐ Partial; Quantity _____

_____

(Signature)

_____

(Name Printed)

_____

(Date)

_____

(Title)

SEND TWO COMPLETE DECK SAMPLES AND PROOF OF MAILING WITH INVOICE.

CHECKLIST 69 Card Pack Order/Inquiry Record

Card Pack Name: _____ Frequency: _____ CPM: _____

Issue Date	Quantity	Cost	Goal ($ or Number of Inquiries)	Orders/Inquiries per Week					Returns	Net Orders/ Inquiries
				Week 1	Week 2	Week 3	Week 4	Week 5 and Later		

Note: Use a separate record for each card pack.

135

A	B	C	D	E
Number of Packages Mailed per Month (000s)	Estimated Price per Thousand Packages Mailed	Brokerage Commission per Thousand Mailed	Net Revenue per Thousand Pieces Mailed	Total Revenue

Column D = Column B – Column C.

Column E = Column A × Column D.

CHECKLIST 71   Insert Program Analysis

Insert Program Name	Description of Audience	Number of Names Available per Month	Cost per Thousand ($)	Size and Weight Limits	Available From	Decision: Yes or No

CHECKLIST 72 Insert Schedule

Insert Name	Key[a] Qty[b] JAN	Key Qty FEB	Key Qty MAR	Key Qty APR	Key Qty MAY	Key Qty JUN	Key Qty JUL	Key Qty AUG	Key Qty SEP	Key Qty OCT	Key Qty NOV	Key Qty DEC	Total Quantity

[a]Key code number.

[b]Quantity of insert pieces.

CHECKLIST 73   Insert Results Analysis

Insert Name	Goal ($)	Key Code Number	Quantity	CPM	Date of First Response	Week 1 Net	Week 2 Net	Week 3 Net	Week 4 Net	Week 5 Net	Total to Date

CHECKLIST 74 Account Analysis

Company: _____

Address: _____

City: _____ State: _____ Zip: _____

Phone: _____ Fax: _____

Contact Names	Title	Phone
1.		
2.		
3.		
4.		
5.		
6.		
7.		
8.		
9.		
10.		

(Checklists 74 through 77 adapted from materials supplied by Telequest, Ft. Worth, Texas.)

Name	Market Share	Marketing Method	Strengths/Weaknesses
1.			
2.			
3.			
4.			
5.			

CHECKLIST 76 Audience Analysis

Customer Profile: _____

_____

_____

_____

_____

1.	Size of potential market?
2.	Number of current customers
3.	How acquired?
4.	How often do they buy?
5.	What are forms of payment?

1.   What is the source, size, and description of the lists we will use?

2.   Who is writing the script?

3.   Who approves the script?

4.   Start-up date?

5.   Length of campaign?

6.   Is fulfillment required?

7.   At what level (number of hours, number of orders) do we need to function, and how soon do we plan to get there?

8.   What training materials are available, and who will supply them?

CHECKLIST 78   Inbound Telemarketing Project Checklist

	Completed	Comments
1. Project Objectives Clarified		
2. Product Information Obtained		
3. Dates for Calling (Establish time frames)		
4. Special 800 Number Assigned (Set up and test lines)		
5. Training		
Establish training dates		
Review training materials		
Staff or nonstaff trainer?		
Are desk references needed?		
Develop benefit profiles		
Number of telemarketers to be trained		
Review call strategy and objectives with trainer		
Materials to trainer		
Input to supervisor for call monitoring		
Pretraining materials to TM reps		
6. Prepare and Distribute Project Overview		
7. Draw Information Flow Chart		

(Checklists 78 through 79 adapted from materials supplied by Telespectrum, Inc., Annapolis, Maryland.)

	Completed	Comments
8. Write Guide and Get Approvals		
Creative/planning sessions as needed		
Decide on qualifying questions		
Decide on data questions		
Determine which results should be tracked		
9. Online Record Storage (Establish parameters for data storage)		
10. Design Project Output		
Labels		
Airbills/packing slips		
Credit card authorization forms		
Diskettes		
Personalized letters/forms		
Lead forms		
11. Design All Desired Reports		
Determine frequency of reports		
Determine statistics desired		
Design summary reports		
12. Design Expense Reports		
Call duration report		
Output tracking report (labels, letters, etc.)		

	Completed	Comments
Transmission tracking reports		
Postage reports		
13. Design Internal Quality Report		
Determine frequency of reports		
Determine statistics desired		
Design summary reports		
14. Fulfillment		
Set up inventory procedures		
Set up reorder points		
Replenish postal account at PO		
15. Order Processing		
Design special invoices, if necessary		
Set up order-processing procedures		
Credit card authorizations		
Purchase order verification		
Reconciliation reports		
Transmission of orders		
16. Programming		
Review guide design		
Review output design		

	Completed	Comments
17. Reviews		
Review all paths for proper coding		
Review data capture		
Review information storage procedures		
Review guide with supervisor		
18. Test Production and Reports		
Test guide in "live" mode		
Test output reports		
Revise and rerun as necessary		
19. First Day Live		
Monitor calls with client		
Feedback to telemarketers and programmer		
Review results		
Test 800 number		
20. Monitor Ongoing Progress		
Monitor calls		
Input to/feedback from telemarketers and supervisors		
Qualitative feedback to client		
21. Project Completion		
Summary reports		
Terminate project		

	Completed	Comments
1. Project Objectives Clarified		
2. Product Information Obtained		
3. Dates for Calling		
Establish time frames		
Number of hours required		
4. Acquire Leads and/or Numbers to Be Called		
5. Establish Fields		
First name		
Last name		
Phone		
Address #1		
Address #2		
City		
State		
Zip		
6. Training		
Establish training dates		
Review training materials		
Staff or nonstaff trainer?		
Are desk references needed?		

	Completed	Comments
Develop benefit profiles		
Number of telemarketers to be trained		
Review call strategy and objectives with trainer		
Materials to trainer		
Input to supervisor for call monitoring		
Pretraining materials to telemarketers		
7. Prepare and Distribute Project Overview		
8. Draw Information Flow Chart		
9. Write Guide and Get Approvals		
Creative/planning sessions as needed		
Decide on qualifying questions		
Decide on data questions		
Determine which results should be tracked		
10. Online Record Storage (Establish parameters for data storage)		
11. Design Project Output		
Labels		
Airbills/packing slips		
Credit card authorization forms		

	Completed	Comments
Diskettes		
Personalized letters/forms		
Lead forms		
12. Design All Desired Reports		
Determine frequency of reports		
Determine statistics desired		
Design summary reports		
13. Design Expense Reports		
Call duration report		
Output tracking report (labels, letters, etc.)		
Transmission tracking reports		
Postage reports		
14. Design Internal Quality Report		
Determine frequency of reports		
Determine statistics desired		
Design summary reports		
15. Design Expense Reports		
Call duration report		
Output tracking report (labels, letters, etc.)		
Transmission tracking reports		
Postage reports		

	Completed	Comments
16. Fulfillment		
Set up inventory procedures		
Set up reorder points		
Replenish postal account at PO		
17. Order Processing		
Design special invoices, if necessary		
Set up order processing procedures		
Credit card authorizations		
Purchase order verification		
Reconciliation reports		
Transmission of orders		
18. BRC Processing		
Design data entry screens		
Select criteria for records to be called		
Date range for processing BRCs		
Instructions for what to do with BRCs		
19. Programming		
Review guide design		
Handling leads with no phone numbers		
Review BRC data entry design		
Review output report design		

	Completed	Comments
20. Reviews		
Review all paths for proper coding		
Review data capture		
Review information storage procedures		
Review guide with supervisor		
21. Test Production and Reports		
Test guide in "live" mode		
Test output reports		
Revise and rerun as necessary		
22. First Day Live		
Monitor calls with client		
Feedback to telemarketers and programmer		
Review results		
Test 800 number		
23. Monitor Ongoing Progress		
Monitor calls		
Input to/feedback from telemarketers and supervisors		
Qualitative feedback to client		
24. Project Completion		
Summary reports		
Terminate project		

CHECKLIST 80   Telemarketing Contact Record

Telemarketer Name/ID _____

Name _____ Title _____

Company _____

Address _____

City _____ State _____ Zip_____

Phone _____ Extension_____ Fax_____

Last Result: ☐ Sale ☐ Upgrade ☐ Cross Sale ☐ Information Request

☐ Call Back: When _____; ☐ No Interest

Follow-Up: Standard Packages ☐ 1; ☐ 2; ☐ 3

☐ Special Letter _____

_____

_____

_____

Best Time to Call: _____ Length of Last Call: _____

Contact Date	Items Sold	Value ($)	Comments	Next Contact Date

(Checklist 80 adapted from materials supplied by Bayley, Leighton & Ryan, New York, New York.)

PART III
Managing Creativity in Direct Marketing

- **6 Checklists for Direct Marketing Formats and Art**
- **4 Checklists for Copy and Production**

6 Checklists for Direct Marketing Formats and Art

Format refers to the size and physical appearance of the advertisement. Format decisions are usually made within the confines of a budget. Certain formats are more effective with some offers and will come to mind at an early stage when planning a marketing campaign. *Layout* refers to the visual appearance of a particular format and is the responsibility of the art director or designer.

CREATIVE FORMATS: RANKED BY COST

Following is a list of formats, starting with the least expensive and progressing to the most expensive:

1. Classified ads

2. Space ads (from small to large)

3. Package inserts

4. Card packs

5. Simple mailing pieces:

   —Double postcard

   —Self-mailer

   —One-color brochure

6. "Standard" mailing package (outer envelope, letter, brochure, order form)

7. "Luxury" mailing package (oversized envelope, full-color materials, personalization, jumbo brochures)

8. "Lavish" special mailing (extraordinarily expensive package; cost is secondary to impact)

The principle that should be observed is to use the most cost-effective format for any particular offer. This is easier said than done. If the product you are selling has a potentially large market, then it is wise to test different formats to find the one that is most effective. The following comments are intended as a guide to choosing formats.

Classified Ads   This is a low-cost way to reach many different types of audiences: consumers, hobbyists, technical people, and so forth. A carefully planned classified ad campaign in appropriate media can generate a surprisingly large number of inquiries that become the basis of a mailing list.

Space Ads   Small space ads can work like classified ads to generate inquiries. They can also generate orders if not too much description is needed for the product. Larger space ads can both generate inquiries and do a complete selling job, depending on how much space is used. Some magazine publishers permit bind-in business reply cards (BRCs) next to full-page ads to make response especially easy.

Package Inserts   Part II explained package inserts in detail. (See Checklists 72 and 73.) They are useful to test products or markets before engaging in a full-scale campaign. For example, if a package insert in an L. L. Bean package program provided acceptable sales, then it would make sense to test the mailing list from the same company.

Card Packs   Card packs usually cost the same as package inserts if you look at the CPM. However, most card packs have higher circulations than the minimums required by a package insert program, so the total cost is greater. Card packs can be used to test products and potential mailing lists (the card pack mailing list is often available for rental separately) or to generate sales. Some companies use card packs almost exclusively as their mail-order sales medium.

Simple Mailing Pieces   These can range from a simple double postcard to a one- or two-page brochure or letter-brochure combination. A self-mailer, if not too elaborate in design, color, or stock, would also fall in this class. For many products—especially if they are promoted to a highly targeted mailing list or to your own house list of customers—this format can be very effective.

"Standard" Mailing Package   Actually, there is no "standard" mailing package, but the commonly used #10 outer envelope containing a letter, brochure, and order card, is used so widely that it qualifies as a standard format. Much creativity can be exercised in its creation, and because it is used so much, it should be high on your list of format choices.

"Luxury" Mailing Package   You will have your own definition of luxury, but most would agree that such packages use a lot of color, oversized envelopes, high-quality paper, personalization, and several prospect-involvement devices: bonus stamps, rub-off cards of winning numbers, seals, and the like. This type of package is usually the domain of large users of direct mail, such as book, magazine, and software publishers. You must have a large potential audience even to consider the up-front costs of creating such a package.

"Lavish" Mailing Packages

These mailing packages are even more costly—per piece—than the luxury packages previously described. However, they are often used for relatively small mailings. Usually they are so out of the ordinary that they no longer qualify as mailings. Sending an autographed baseball in a gift package to promote some sports offer could be an example. A small company can sometimes afford an effort like this to reach several hundred prospects.

CHOOSING THE FORMAT

No hard-and-fast rules on choosing a format will apply in all cases, but **Checklist 81,** Continuum of Format Choices, may help you select a format. The vertical column at the left suggests low-budget situations; the one on the right indicates high-budget situations. The five boxes show where on the scale of choices you believe your product fits.

You can quickly see from your checks whether the marks are skewed toward one direction or the other, and the form will help you in making a better choice of format *budget.* After you feel comfortable with a budget, then you can decide on a particular format.

Art Decisions

You may have a staff artist or designer working full- or part-time for you, or you may depend on several free-lancers to do the work on a project-by-project basis. There are pros and cons to each situation:

AN IN-HOUSE ARTIST OR DESIGNER:

- Knows your routines and standards.
- Is available all the time.
- Can work closely with writers and marketing people.
- Is costly if there are not sufficient projects to occupy him or her.
- Can become bored in time and produce routine designs.

A FREE-LANCE ARTIST OR DESIGNER:

- Is usually less costly than a full-time staffer.
- Means a greater range of talents to choose from.
- Eliminates overhead costs of benefits and so on.
- Requires more explanation or instruction on jobs.
- May not be available in an emergency.

Checklist 82, In-house/Freelance Selector, is a simple way to visualize whether you are better off with a freelancer or an in-house artist. If you have more *yes* than *no* answers, go with the in-house person.

Checklist 83, Freelance Artist/Designer Information, can be transferred to a 5 × 8 filecard for easy reference. It is especially useful if you have a wide variety of art and design work ranging from simple, one-color ads to elaborate full-color pieces. You can pick the artist most suited for a particular assignment quickly, or find a back-up if the one you want is unavailable at the time you need the service.

Whether you decide on a staff or a free-lance designer, you can use **Checklist 84,** Art and Design Requisition, to assign jobs. Put all the specifications down as completely as possible. In the long run, this will save time in revising jobs, and, in the case of free-lancers, it will eliminate fees for "author's alterations" (AAs).

At the same time, you can start getting your cost estimates. In case your preliminary estimates are too low, you will have time to revise the assignments and ask for something less costly. **Checklist 85,** Production Estimating, should be filled in as soon as possible. This can be handled by a marketing staff member working with outside vendors or, in larger companies, by turning over the whole job to a production person.

Finally, the finished art represents a great investment in time and money. Often the mechanical can be reused as is or revised to reflect changes in price or specifications. It is important that you have an accurate and up-to-date art inventory. **Checklist 86,** Art Inventory Record, should be considered a vital record and entrusted to a responsible person.

If you produce many similar products (a book publisher is a good example), it is quite easy to fall into a routine of using the same format over and over to promote these products. This saves time for everyone, but it can result in a sameness of approach and appearance that can depress sales after a while.

Using the format decision tools in this chapter can help you add variety and interest to your advertisement without necessarily going over your budget.

4 Checklists for Copy and Production

All the planning for a direct mail campaign will be unavailing if the copy—the ultimate selling message going out to your public—is weak, is ineffective, or misses the point. It is not unusual for marketing managers to oversee all the details of a campaign and then to either neglect the copy or meddle in its creation to such an extent that it loses all sales appeal.

The bottom line for any advertisement is how well it answers the reader's question: "What's in it for me?" Your reader is interested in how the product will satisfy some need—business, personal, or whatever. Everything else is secondary. This section is written especially for marketing managers. It will show you how to get the best sales copy possible. Copywriters and others will find these checklists and forms useful also.

PRELIMINARY STEPS

The following steps may seem obvious to some advertising professionals, but it is little short of amazing how often they are neglected.

1. **Research.** Everything known about the product or service should be available in written form. This should include everything from what the product does, to how it looks, to how much it weighs, and any other details. Nothing should be considered irrelevant at this point. Collect as much information on competitors' products or services as you can for comparison purposes.

2. **Define the main benefits.** This is a good time for marketing managers, salespeople, copywriters, and others to meet and agree on the benefits that will be stressed in all sales messages. What is the most important need satisfied by this product or service? Don't be misled into thinking that a clever copywriter will come up with a cute slogan that will sell.

3. **List all the selling points.** The selling points show how the product or service achieves these benefits. The more selling points you have, the better, even if you do not use them all in your advertising.

4. **Repeat Steps 2–3 for secondary benefits.** At this same meeting, agree on the secondary benefits and selling points.

5. **Agree on a budget.** Note that we did not say "agree on a format." A more effective piece for the money will often result if you let the creative

people—copywriters, art directors, and designers—have freedom to work within the constraints of a budget, rather than being forced into a preconceived format.

6. **Let the creative people create.** Avoid interfering in the creative process. If you've hired competent people, they will give you a competent piece containing all the main and secondary benefits previously agreed on. Nothing can drain life and spontaneity from a piece of copy faster than the suggestions and revisions of a "committee of experts."

The creation of copy will be easier if you use **Checklist 87,** Copy Benefits. Take it to the meeting and fill it in completely, using additional pages if need be. Later, all advertising pieces can be tested against this road map to see whether the copy is on track.

COPY ASSIGNMENTS

At this point you can use **Checklist 88,** Requisition for Direct Response Campaign. The product or products to be sold in the advertisement are identified, and all the research material collected should be made part of the requisition package sent to the creative director or copy chief.

The budget is for the creative work and all the expenses leading to finished art or mechanicals ready for production. The campaign description can define in general terms what kind of piece is envisioned or budgeted. Is it a low-cost black-and-white flyer or an elaborate four-color campaign? Is it going to be different from anything previously done, or will it be modeled on an ongoing piece? This is where you give direction to the creative people.

If the format is tested and fairly standard, then fill in the boxes describing what sort of letter or other campaign elements are desired. The due dates establish deadlines so the creative process can be monitored and mailing dates met.

The creative director or copy chief can use **Checklist 89,** Direct Mail Copy Assignment, to assign the various jobs to the copywriters involved. It is really a traffic control form and should be made out in duplicate, one for the copywriter and one for the copy chief for follow-up, to make sure deadlines are met.

The target mailing lists for the campaign are useful for the copywriter, because they might suggest a tone for the piece. It is important for the writer to identify with the audience, and this information is vital for that purpose.

If the ads requisitioned are for space ads or card decks, use **Checklist 90,** Space Ad/Deck Copy Assignment. This form is similar to the previous one, except that it gives specific information on ad sizes, screens, and other elements that must be considered.

COPY TIPS No copy should ever be considered final, even if it is working successfully. If you have a mailing package that is working well, consider it a "control" package and develop variants for testing. You might want to test a different benefit; what you think is important may not be the prime benefit in the reader's mind.

When writing copy, try to observe the rule of the inverted pyramid that is used in writing news stories. It is more than likely that you will need copy on the same product to fit different spaces. You may need a full-page ad in a main magazine, a quarter-page ad in another publication, and a paragraph in a catalog, perhaps. If you write so that the main benefit is first and lesser benefits follow, it will be easy to produce all types of ads from a single creative effort. There will be no need to recreate different copy to fit different spaces.

The following copy formula—HEY! YOU! SEE? SO!—was inspired by Walter S. Campbell's *Writing Non-Fiction* (Boston: The Writer, Inc, 1944). Every piece of persuasive writing, whether it is a direct mail piece or a love letter, is most effective when it follows this four-part formula to some degree.

HEY! In the beginning you've got to attract the reader's attention in some fashion. You don't actually yell *Hey!* but the effect is the same. On the envelope, in the headline, or at the top of a space ad, you must make some statement that attracts attention and makes the reader want to know more. This statement is invariably the main benefit and the promise it gives the reader of saving time or money, gaining success in business or personal matters, or preventing something undesirable from happening.

YOU! Here is where inexperienced copywriters (and frequently top corporate executives) make a big mistake. They like to talk about their company, their reputation, and the like. As soon as you attract the reader's attention with the main benefit, you should immediately follow up with a "you" pitch. The reader is not much interested in what you say about yourself or your company, but is immensely interested in himself or herself. Show how the product will benefit the reader specifically.

SEE? Now come the explanations. Here is where all your selling points come into play. The reader will want to know clearly what the product does, how it does it, why it is a bargain, whether it is guaranteed to work, and a host of other details. List these thoughts in order of importance and describe them clearly, vividly, and with feeling in the ad. These are the reasons to buy, and they should be numerous, interesting, and convincing.

SO! This is the clincher, in which you ask for an order. Surprisingly enough, many otherwise good salespeople fall down on this score, whether they are selling in person or via the printed word. You must ask the reader for an order or for some action. Make it easy. Repeat it often, and don't forget to remind the reader again of your returns and guarantee policies.

Whether you are a copywriter, copy chief, or marketing manager who must approve copy, if you apply this four-part formula the chances are very good you will have an above-average number of mail-order successes.

CHECKLIST 81   Continuum of Format Choices

Low Budget for Creative Format	Low ✔	Slightly Low ✔	Average ✔	Slightly High ✔	High ✔	High Budget for Creative Format
1. Product, low price						1. Product, high price
2. Small lists						2. Large lists
3. Small target market						3. Large target market
4. "Risky" product or idea						4. Tested product or idea
5. Limited budget						5. Adequate budget
6. Untested lists or market						6. Tested lists or market
7. No in-house list of buyers						7. In-house list of buyers
8. Other						8. Other

Requirements	Yes	No
Is knowledge of in-house procedures essential?		
Is detailed knowledge of product necessary?		
Is on-the-job availability important?		
Is close work required with in-house staff?		
Are salary and benefits budgeted for a full timer?		
Is enough work available to keep an in-house person busy full time?		
Can other departments use in-house person and share expenses?		
Is person responsible for other tasks (art inventory, etc.)		
Is space available for in-house artist/designer?		
Is furniture and equipment available for in-house person?		

CHECKLIST 83   Freelance Artist/Designer Information

Name: _____

Address: _____

Phone: _____   Fax: _____

☐ Independent or ☐ Studio

Studio Affiliation: _____

Recommended by: _____ Phone: _____

How are jobs charged? _____☐ per hour ☐ per job

Does he/she work on weekends? ☐ Yes   ☐ No

Turn around speed: ☐ Slow   ☐ Average   ☐ Quick

Portfolio evaluation and comments: _____

_____

_____

_____

_____

_____

CHECKLIST 84   Art and Design Requisition

From: Art Director

To: _____   Date: _____

Product: _____   Code No.: _____ Price:_____

Due Date: _____   Mail Date: _____

Media	Specs
☐ Space Ad	
Size	
Colors	
Special Requirements	
☐ Mailing Piece(s)	
☐ Letter	
☐ Brochure	
☐ Envelope	
☐ BRC/BRE	
☐ Other	
☐ Postcard	
Size	
Colors	
Special Requirements	

Special Instructions: _____

_____

_____

CHECKLIST 85   Production Estimating

Campaign: _____

Quantity: _____ Mail Date: _____

Campaign Element	Estimate A	Estimate B	Estimate C
Printing			
Outer envelope			
Reply envelope			
Reply card			
Letter			
Brochure 1			
Brochure 2			
Other elements			
Lists			
House lists			
Outside list rental			
Merge/purge			
Magnetic tape			
Labels			
Other			
Lettershop Services			
Inserting			
Labeling			
Personalization			
Metering			
Sort/tie/mail			
Other			
Postage			
First-class			
Bulk			
Net postage			
TOTAL COSTS:			

CHECKLIST 86 Art Inventory Record

Product: _____   Code No: _____   Price: _____

Media Type	Available in what form?	Location	Date Last Used
(Space ad, postcard, flyer, envelope, BRE, etc.)	(Original art, repro, film, mechanical, etc.)	(Files, printer, client, archives)	

CHECK ALL PRICES AND SPECS BEFORE REUSING

Main Benefit	Selling Points
(What need does this product or service satisfy?) 1.	(How does this product or service satisfy this need? How does it satisfy this need better than everything else that is on the market?) 1. 2. 3. 4. 5.

Secondary Benefits	Selling Points
2.	1. 2. 3.
3.	1. 2. 3.
4.	1. 2. 3.

CHECKLIST 88   Requisition for Direct Response Campaign

To: Creative Director or Copy Chief   From: Marketing Management

Product: _____ Budget:_____

Campaign Description: _____

_____

_____

(If specific formats or pieces are requested, fill in below.)

Component	✔	Description	Copy Due	Art Due	Mechanical Due
Letter					
Circular					
Envelope					
BRC or BRE					
Lift letter					
Premium flyer					
Other					

From: Creative Director or Copy Chief   Date: _____

To: Copy Staff

Product: _____   Code No: _____ Price: _____

Due Date: _____   Mail Date: _____

Description: _____

_____

_____

Target Market (identify mailing lists):

Secondary Market:

Copy Format/Special Instructions:

CHECKLIST 90   Space Ad/Deck Copy Assignment

From: Creative Director or Copy Chief   Date: _____

To: Copy Staff   ☐ Space Ad   ☐ Deck

Product: _____   Code No: _____ Price:_____

Publication: _____   Issue/ Date: _____

Copy Due Date: _____   Insertion Order Date: _____

Mechanical Due Date: _____   Ad/Card Size:_____

Line Screen:_____   Promotion Key No.: _____

Description: _____

_____

Target Market:

Secondary Market:

Copy Format/Special Instructions:

Send insertion order and mechanical or negatives to:

PART IV
After the Campaign: Back-End Direct Marketing

- **2 Checklists for Inquiry Handling**
- **5 Checklists for Back-End Analysis**

2 Checklists for Inquiry Handling

Not every response in the business of direct response is a sale. Sometimes, a prospect is unconvinced and needs more information or simply is not ready to make a purchase decision. Woe to the marketer who contacts prospects and, when a sale is not immediately consummated, assumes that no sale is possible.

Telemarketers often are judged strictly on the sales they make. When a customer asks for more information or otherwise indicates some interest in the product or service but declines immediate acceptance, the telemarketer may terminate the call because he or she has no instructions about how to handle an inquiry. Management may think that it is better to end the call than to have a telemarketer take the time to send a letter or even forward the inquiry to the advertising department.

The first law of inquiry handling is to be prepared. *Always anticipate that someone will ask for information.* Even though your space ad is prepared for the sole intention of generating orders, you may get a large number of information requests. When this happens, there is often a scramble to find an existing brochure or catalog to send and to write a letter.

There are many types of inquiries, and you should have different types of responses depending on the ordering potential of the person making the inquiry. For example, if you receive a reader service card (bingo card) as the result of a space ad, you know that the prospect can fill out a single card and generate a response from every advertiser in the magazine, without paying postage. Very little effort on the part of the prospect is required, so therefore what you send to that unqualified prospect will be your least costly follow-up.

On the other hand, when a prospect writes a letter asking for information, that activity required time, energy, and postage. That person was willing to expend effort and may therefore be a better prospect than the person who filled out the bingo card. This is not an absolute standard, but when nothing else is known about the prospect, the amount of effort expended to contact your company is one way to qualify an inquiry.

Checklist 91, Type of Inquiry Follow-Up, will help you establish exactly what your inquiry response procedures will be. Following is an example of how this checklist would be used.

Product: Home Workshop   **Media:** Popular Mechanics   **Date:** February issue

Response Item or Activity	Exists (✓) or Needs to Be Created	Source of Inquiry			
		Bingo Card	Coupon	Letter or Telephone Call	Request to Telemarketer
Envelope	✓	✓	✓	✓	✓
Letter	**Need**	✓	✓	✓	✓
Direct mail piece	✓			✓	✓
Mini-catalog	✓		✓		
Catalog	✓				
Price list	✓	✓			
Follow-up telemarketing call				✓	✓

TELEMARKETING INQUIRY FOLLOW-UP

When your telemarketers call customers who do not want to make an immediate decision, are they instructed to terminate the call, to promise to call again, or to assure customers that information will be mailed to them? There is no single best response. Telemarketing is an expensive medium, and you might decide for a particular campaign that when a customer refuses to make a decision on the spot, it is not worth it to initiate a follow-up.

There are several factors to weigh before making this decision to follow up or not to follow up. How important is the customer to you? If you are selling to business and industry and your prospect universe is small, it is probably worthwhile to send information to any prospect who expresses interest in your product or service. A customer who is on the fence about making a purchase decision may really want more information. Can you afford to alienate a potential customer? If yours is a consumer product, it may be inefficient to hamper your telemarketers with follow-up responsibilities.

The best course may be to test different responses and see which is the best alternative. Having a telemarketer write up a request for more information may reduce the total number of prospects to be called each day. Can you estimate the number of sales you will lose from that activity?

In the following example, it takes 12 calls (Column B) to make one sale ($100):

Product price: $100   **Cost of follow-up materials and postage: $1**

A Average Number of Calls Lost per Day	B Average Number of Calls per Sale	C Average Number of Inquiries per Day	D Average Number of Inquiries per Sale
6	12	15	20

If your telemarketers interrupt their sales calling to answer inquiries, you will lose six calls a day (Column A). Six calls represents one-half of a sale, so you will lose $50/day. If each telemarketer answers 15 inquiries per day (Column C), and on the average it takes 20 inquiries to generate one sale, the 15 inquiries represent three-fourths of a sale per day (Column C ÷ Column D), or a gain of $75/day. Therefore, answering inquiries will gain $75/day/telemarketer and lose $50/day/telemarketer from lost direct sales, or a final gain of $25/day/telemarketer. To figure profit, subtract the cost of sending materials to prospects (15 inquiries × $1 = $15), for a net profit of $10/day/telemarketer. In this case, answering inquiries would be more profitable than ignoring them.

Checklist 92, Income (Loss) from Telemarketers Handling Inquiries, is a spreadsheet you can use to analyze your alternatives.

5 Checklists for Back-End Analysis

The "back end" in a direct response operation is analogous to order fulfillment, but from a marketing point of view as it involves analysis of the order rather than the physical tasks of picking, packing, and shipping the product. The back end is what you do with a received order to increase sales, ensure customer satisfaction, and improve mailing lists.

INCREASING SALES

As a marketer, you have several options for gaining incremental sales through the back end, at little extra cost. These back-end sales can often mean the difference between profit and loss on a list or campaign. Back-end sales should always be tracked. **Checklist 93,** Back-End Sales Analysis—Quantities Sent, and **Checklist 94,** Back-End Sales Analysis—Orders Received, will assist you in the vital task of tracking monthly back-end sales figures.

Package Inserts

Here are some suggestions of items you might include with a product as package inserts:

1. Direct mail piece

2. Coupon

3. Special offer

4. Price list

5. Mini-catalog

6. Full catalog

7. Deck-mail package

8. Marketing research questionnaire

9. Free sample of another product

10. Order form

Back-end sales will lag behind the promotion efforts. For example, a catalog inserted in a January shipment will probably start producing orders in February or later. Tracking the quantities mailed in shipments with resulting orders will show which inserts are most productive. You can also test one type of insert against another by doing an A/B split. In this instance, an A/B split would be to alternate two different inserts into shipments of the same product. It is important to keep alternating inserts as the product is shipped and to make sure that the same number of each insert is mailed. This A/B method means that you are randomly selecting customers, which is important for an unbiased test.

Retail Invoice Envelope Advertising

Another back-end sales method is to use the flap of your retail invoice envelope to sell another product. Department stores and credit card companies use this sales technique routinely, and there is nothing to prevent a smaller company from doing the same thing. If you are not now doing this, try to work a deal with your accounts receivable department in which the direct response department pays for the small incremental cost of adding a flap to the regular retail payment envelope. Because the billing department sends out the invoice, your ad requires no postage. And, of course, when the customers pay the bill, they put your flap-order form into the billing envelope, for which they pay the postage. This envelope direct response device is known by many different names, two of which are *hot potato* and *bang tail.*

Depending on the sophistication of the shipping and billing departments, the package inserts and retail payment envelopes could have different inserts for the various products being shipped. If your shipping department can handle having separate inserts for different products, you can target your sales effort very effectively. For example, if your target market is engineers and you have different products for civil, mechanical, electrical, electronic, and chemical engineers, it would make sense to send discipline-specific materials to each type of engineer. If, however, many different inserts would slow down your warehouse operation to a point where the added sales might not compensate for the extra time incurred to insert the items, you will have to find products that cut across disciplines so that all the recipients would be interested in them.

In **Checklist 95,** Part I, Column 1 shows the product being billed to the customer. If you are able to segment customers by discipline, interest level, or product type, then you could select products A to F to be stuffed into the retail envelope or put on the bang tail. However, if the retail invoice envelope is mailed to all customers and cannot be segmented, then you could use a generic insert, the same for all customers (Part II).

ENSURING CUSTOMER SATISFACTION

What can you do to make sure that your customers are pleased with the product they receive? Here is an opportunity to cement customer loyalty and increase sales. You could insert a letter asking for suggestions or giving a toll-free number for customer service or offering free postage if the item needs to be returned. The company's returns policy, of course, may dictate what you can offer. Whatever it is that you do for a customer, let the customer know what you are doing and how it will save them money, save them time, make them money, or provide some other benefit. Customers appreciate having companies pay attention to their needs.

Checklist 96, Product Inserts, is for you to review different products you ship and decide which insert would be appropriate.

When a customer places an order from your direct response campaign, they may pay for the product in advance, pay for the product when billed, return the product, or not pay for the product at all. Some companies offer to pay the postage and handling costs if a customer pays in advance of shipping the order. When a customer does pay in advance, you will receive less revenue by not billing the customer for postage and handling, but you will reduce billing costs and the amount of bad debts. Only your accounting department can tell you whether this is a profitable strategy. Since the extra cost of postage and handling is a source of customer dissatisfaction in many direct mail industries, offering free postage and handling for prepaid orders could increase sales. It is probably worth testing.

IMPROVING MAILING LISTS

Whether a customer pays in advance or when billed, that person's name is a valuable addition to your in-house mailing list. The addition of that customer also makes your own list rental business more valuable, because lists of people who buy through direct response are precious commodities.

Returns

Keeping a history of people who return items is important. A customer who purchases from your company and occasionally returns an item could be an active buyer. If a person continually orders products and returns them, their names should be flagged and, after a predetermined number of returns, deleted from your mailings. You may want to create a list of people to whom you do not wish to mail offerings and to include that list in your merge/purge sequence for every mailing.

Bad Debts

Bad debts cost a company more than the manufacturing cost of a product ordered but not paid for. Most companies have dunning procedures that continue to rebill customers for six or more times until the unpaid bill is written off, given to a collection agency, or both. Even more important is getting the nonpaying customer off your in-house buyer's lists so that you do not continue to contact that person with yet another offer.

Some bad debts are the result of a misunderstanding—the customer thought he or she was getting a particular product for a particular purpose and, for whatever reason, the customer does not think the product ordered lived up to expectations. If the customer has a history of buying your product and paying for it, you probably will want to come to an accommodation rather than lose that customer.

There are other reasons for bad debts—some forgivable, some not— but those people who actively try to cheat your company by ordering items and having no intention to pay are especially costly to your bottom line. One common ploy is to use different first initials or first names when ordering different products through direct response. If your computer program can spot a pattern of abuse, you should be able to keep that person's name off your list. If your computer program is not that sophisticated, it would be worthwhile, every few months, for someone to check your bad-debt file manually and look for bad-debt patterns.

Tracking Out-of-House Lists

Just as you should be aware of return patterns and bad-debt patterns on your in-house lists, you should be keeping a history of outside lists as well. If a list has an unusual number of bad debts, consider abandoning it.

Every aspect of customer contact has potential for increasing sales, ensuring customer satisfaction, and improving your buyers lists. Customer service, which is not discussed in this book, is another area where you can find many sales opportunities. Look around your company. Wherever there is customer contact, the direct response department should be able to find ways to gain from them.

Checklist 97 will be useful in keeping track of list history.

CHECKLIST 91 Type of Inquiry Follow-Up

Product: _____ Media: _____

Issue Date: _____ Quantity/Circulation: _____

Response Item	Exists (✔) or Needs to Be Created	Source of Inquiry			
		Bingo Card	Coupon	Letter or Telephone Call	Tele-marketer Follow-Up
Envelope					
Letter					
Direct mail piece					
Mini-catalog					
Catalog					
Price list					
Follow-up telemarketing call					

CHECKLIST 92   Income (Loss) from Telemarketers Handling Inquiries

A	B	C	D	E	F	G	H	I
Average Sale	Average Number of Calls Lost for Inquiries per Day	Average Number of Calls per Sale	Average Sales Lost per Day[a]	Average Number of Inquiries per Day	Average Number of Inquiries per Sale	Average Sales per Day from Inquiries[b]	Average Cost of Inquiry	Gain (Loss) from Inquiries[c]

[a](Column B ÷ Column C) × Column A.

[b](Column F ÷ Column E) × Column A.

[c]Column G − Column D − Column H.

CHECKLIST 93 Back-End Sales Analysis—Quantities Sent

Quantities Inserted into Product Shipment, by Month

Insert	Jan	Feb	Mar	Apr	May	Jun	Jul	Aug	Sep	Oct	Nov	Dec	Total
Direct mail brochure													
Coupon													
Special offer													
Price list													
Mini-catalog													
Full catalog													
Deck-mail package													
Research													
Sample													
Order form[a]													

[a]Refers to a stand-alone ordering device. All other categories include an ordering device.

CHECKLIST 94 Back-End Sales Analysis—Orders Received

Orders (Responses) Received, by Month

Insert	Jan	Feb	Mar	Apr	May	Jun	Jul	Aug	Sep	Oct	Nov	Dec	Total
Direct mail piece													
Coupon													
Special offer													
Price list													
Mini-catalog													
Full catalog													
Deck–mail package													
Research													
Sample													
Order form													

Product to Be Billed	Products to Be Included					
	A ✔	B ✔	C ✔	D ✔	E ✔	F ✔
(I) **Targeted Mailings**						
1:						
2:						
3:						
(II) **Untargeted Mailings**						
1:						
2:						
3:						

Product

Item	A	B	C	D	E	F
Direct mail piece						
Coupon						
Special offer						
Price list						
Mini-catalog						
Catalog						
Card pack						
Market research						
Free sample						
Order form						
Toll-free number						
Letter						
Customer service brochure						

CHECKLIST 97 List History

List Name: _____

Broker: _____

CPM: _____

Selects Available: _____

List Owner: _____

Total Quantity: _____

Source: _____

Date	Quantity Mailed	Nixes	Number of Orders	Orders ($)	Number of Returns	Percentage of Returns	Number of Bad Debts	Bad Debts ($)	Percentage of Bad Debts	Total Percentage of Bad Debts and Returns	Reuse List? (Yes / No)

APPENDIX
Marketing Arithmetic

■ *2 Checklists for Marketing Calculations*

2 Checklists for Marketing Calculations

In marketing, there are many numbers for which managers may be accountable. Some firms require elaborate analyses, including return on investment (ROI), return on assets (ROA), and many more. We have included ROI and ROA and pricing considerations for your information, but for the purposes of this book, here are the three analyses you will probably find most helpful: gross margin, break-even, and campaign profit and loss analysis.

CALCULATING GROSS MARGIN

Gross margin is a measure that tells management (and the accountants) whether the product you plan to offer for sale can make a profit. Gross margin is the amount of money generated by a sale after discounts have been allowed, returns have been subtracted, and the cost of creating (or purchasing) the product has been subtracted. In other words, gross margin dollars are what pays your salary, the expenses of the company, and the expenses of your campaign and provides the profit. **Checklist 98,** Calculating Gross Margin, will help you with this formula.

Gross margin may be expressed in dollars or as a percentage. Often, a company may establish a minimum gross margin percentage that products must meet in order to be sold by your company. If a product's gross margin isn't high enough to meet company profitability guidelines, it can never be a profitable product for your company—no matter how successfully it is sold. The following is a simple table to help you determine a product's gross margin:

	A	B	C	D	E
Product	List Price	Discounts	Net Price[a]	Cost of Goods Sold	Gross Margin[b] ($)
A	$45.00	$15.00	$30.00	$10.00	$20.00
B	40.00	15.00	25.00	10.00	15.00
C	51.00	17.00	34.00	10.00	24.00

[a]Column A - Column B.

[b]Column C - Column D.

To figure gross margin as a percentage, divide the gross margin dollars by the net price. You can make your calculations based on a single unit or on the total sales of an entire product. Just make sure you use one calculation base or the other, not both simultaneously.

	A	B	C	D
	Net Price	Cost of Goods Sold	Gross Margin[a] ($)	Gross Margin[b] (%)
A	$30.00	$10.00	$20.00	66.6%
B	25.00	10.00	15.00	60
C	34.00	10.00	24.00	71

[a]Column A - Column B.

[b]Column C ÷ Column A.

BREAK-EVEN ANALYSIS

The break-even point (BEP) is the level of sales at which a product's total revenue equals its total cost. There are several different methods to figure break-even; two of them are shown here. The first method uses a formula. It is useful when you are setting up a campaign and need to know the point at which your project will start showing real profit potential—in other words, when it stops losing money. The second method, the pro-forma profit and loss (P&L) statement, helps you assess the specific profitability of each campaign. The formula method is useful in the planning stages. The latter method, the P&L, requires isolating all campaign cost components and tracking them carefully.

Formula Method

The break-even analysis formula shows how many units you must sell to cover the fixed costs assigned to a particular product. Each sale you make contributes something toward fixed costs. *Fixed costs* are those expenses that are incurred no matter how many units are produced. Fixed costs include rent, property taxes, insurance, management salaries, other overhead, and depreciation. The number you need to calculate is the total fixed cost (TFC) that has been assigned to the specific percentage of the budgeted sales for a company. It could be 2 percent or $1/2$ percent or much less; it could be 50 percent or more.

Here's a hypothetical example to clarify a few concepts. Suppose that Product A will generate 10 percent of all sales for the year. If the fixed costs for the company are $100,000, then the TFC assigned to Product A is $10,000 (10 percent of $100,000). If the sales estimate for Product A is 100,000 units, then each unit sold will return to the company 1/100,000 of the fixed costs assigned to that product ($10,000 ÷ 100,000 = $.10 per unit). Each unit of Product A that is sold returns $.10 toward the fixed costs assigned to Product A. If Product A sells for $10.00, then there is $9.90 per unit that goes to pay other expenses. One of those other expenses is the variable cost.

Variable costs are expenses that depend on the production of the product: manufacturing salaries; raw, processed, and prefabricated materials; packaging; shipping; sales commissions; marketing expenses; and an allowance for bad debts. So another number we need to calculate is the total variable costs (TVC). A companion number is the average variable cost (AVC) per unit, which is found by dividing the TVC by the number of units to be sold. If it costs $30,000 to produce 15,000 units, then we divide $30,000 by 15,000, or $2.00 per unit AVC.

We now know how to figure total fixed costs and average fixed costs and total variable costs and average variable costs. We therefore can add together the total fixed costs and the total variable costs to determine the total cost (TC). Again, to learn the average total cost (ATC), we divide the total cost by the number of units to be sold. To review, here are the parts of the break-even formula:

Average Fixed Costs = Total Fixed Costs ÷ Quantity Sold
Average Variable Cost = Total Variable Costs ÷ Quantity Sold
Total Cost = Total Fixed Costs + Total Variable Costs
Average Total Cost = Total Cost ÷ Quantity Sold

Our goal is to reach break-even as quickly as possible so that our product pays its share of company expenses, all of its campaign expenses, and contributes to the company's profitability.

The next item we need to learn is the fixed cost contribution (FCC) per unit. To do this, take the unit price and subtract from it the average variable cost. What remains can go to pay the fixed costs. Mathematically, this is stated as follows:

Fixed Cost Contribution = Unit Price – Average Variable Cost

The following is a hypothetical example of a product to be sold through direct response with the various relevant costs listed:

Quantity Sold (QS) = 15,000
Unit Price = $10
TFC = $21,000
TVC = $30,000

BEP Formula: TFC ÷ FCC = BEP (in units)
         AVC = TVC ÷ QS = $2
         FCC = Unit Price – AVC = $10 – $2 = $8
         TFC ÷ FCC = $21,000 ÷ $8 = 2,625 units = BEP

At the break-even point, all of the fixed costs have been paid off. Any money collected after the break-even point will go toward paying for the sales campaign, the variable costs, and profit. The fixed cost contribution per unit may be difficult to understand; we use this concept to give a portion of the fixed cost to every unit sold below break-even. When break-even is reached, fixed costs are paid off for this product and we can begin to look toward making a profit.

Pro-Forma Profit and Loss Analysis Method

The second break-even method is the pro-forma profit and loss (P&L) statement for each campaign. It is a critical step in planning and analyzing sales efforts. Try to be realistic; not every campaign will be successful. If you use this P&L method assiduously, it should help you determine when a campaign is working and when it is not.

Checklist 99, Pro-Forma Profit and Loss Analysis, is intended to help you analyze the break-even point for a specific product or service. See the example on page 199.

SETTING PRICES

A pricing decision is based on covering your fixed and variable costs, the break-even point, the profit sought, pricing by your competition, the differentiation between your product and the competition, and the perceived value of your product by the customer.

In order to make a pricing decision, you must analyze results based on various sales estimates. Using a computer spreadsheet program will speed your calculations. One pricing method is as follows:

$$\text{AFC (average fixed cost)} + \text{AVC (average variable cost)} + \text{APU (average profit per unit)} = \text{minimum unit price}$$

You must make sure that all your expenses are included in this formula. This formula provides your minimum price. However, it does not have an allowance for taxes. The actual selling price must also reflect your position in the marketplace vis-à-vis your competition.

You may set any price you think you will be able to command from your customers. However, you should be aware of your competitors' prices. If your product is recognized by your customers to be superior to your competitors', you may be able to establish a higher price. However, it is important to know whether your customer is willing to pay a higher price even for a superior product.

RETURN ON INVESTMENT (ROI)

This calculation is to determine the ratio of net profit (after taxes) to the investment used to make the net profit, multiplied by 100 to eliminate decimals. *Investment* is the dollar resources the firm has paid to establish a project or business. There are two ways to estimate ROI:

1. ROI (%) = Net Profit (after taxes) ÷ Investments × 100

2. ROI (%) = (Net Profit after Taxes ÷ Sales) × (Sales ÷ Investments × 100)

Or, stated another way:

    ROI (%) = Net Profit (%) × Turnover × 100

Using the second method, it is clear that to increase ROI you can:

1. Increase the profit margin (by lowering costs or by charging more)

2. Increase sales

3. Decrease investment

RETURN ON ASSETS (ROA)

ROA (%) = (Net Profit × 100) ÷ Assets

Both ROI and ROA measure how effectively the company is using its resources.

Example of Profit and Loss Analysis

Product: <u>ADVERTISING EXECS DIRECTORY</u> Key: <u>AD AGE AA·101</u> Date: <u>1 / 12 / xx</u>

1.	Sales Price of Goods or Services	$80.00	
2.	Cost of Sales		
	a. Cost of Goods or Services	16.00	
	b. Royalty or License Fees	—	
	c. Handling (Order Processing, Picking, and Packing)	5.00	
	d. Postage / Shipping Expense	3.00	
	e. Premium (Includes Shipping and Handling)	1.00	
	Total Cost of Sales:		$25.00
3.	Overhead (Rent, Utilities, Salaries) (Percentage of #1)	10%	8.00
4.	Estimated Percentage of Returns	5%	
5.	Return Handling Expenses		
	a. Return Postage and Handling (#2c + #2d)	$8.00	
	b. Refurbishing Returned Merchandise (12.5% of #2a)	2.00	
	Total Cost of Handling Returns:		10.00
6.	Chargeable Cost of Returns (#4 × Total Cost of Handling Returns)		.50
7.	Estimated Bad Debt (%)	3%	
8.	Chargeable Cost of Bad Debts (#1 × #7)		2.40
9.	Total Variable Costs (#2 + #3 + #6 + #8)		35.90
10.	Unit Profit after Deducting Variable Costs (#1 – #9)		44.10
11.	Anticipated Return Factor (100% – #4)	97%	
12.	Unit Profit per Order (#10 × #11)		42.78
13.	Credit for Returned Merchandise (#4 × #2a)		.80
14.	Net Profit per Order (#12 + #13)		43.58
15.	Cost per Thousand Contacts (Marketing Expense)	$400—	
16.	Number of Orders per Thousand Needed to Break Even (#15 ÷ #14)		9.2

Source: Adapted from Boise Cascade Envelope Division.

Product	A List Price	B Discounts	C Net Price[a]	D Cost of Goods Sold	E Gross Margin[b] ($)	F Gross Margin[c] (%)
A						
B						
C						
D						
E						
F						
G						
H						

[a]Column A – Column B.
[b]Column C – Column D.
[c]Column E ÷ Column C.

Product: _____ Key: _____ Date: _____

1.	Sales Price of Goods or Services		
2.	Cost of Sales		
	a. Cost of Goods or Services		
	b. Royalty or License Fees		
	c. Handling (Order Processing, Picking, and Packing)		
	d. Postage / Shipping Expense		
	e. Premium (Includes Shipping and Handling)		
Total Cost of Sales:			
3.	Overhead (Rent, Utilities, Salaries) (Percentage of #1)		
4.	Estimated Percentage of Returns		
5.	Return Handling Expenses		
	a. Return Postage and Handling (#2c + #2d)		
	b. Refurbishing Returned Merchandise (12.5% of #2a)		
Total Cost of Handling Returns:			
6.	Chargeable Cost of Returns (#4 × Total Cost of Handling Returns)		
7.	Estimated Bad Debt (%)		
8.	Chargeable Cost of Bad Debts (#1 × #7)		
9.	Total Variable Costs (#2 + #3 + #6 + #8)		
10.	Unit Profit after Deducting Variable Costs (#1 − #9)		
11.	Anticipated Return Factor (100% − #4)		
12.	Unit Profit per Order (#10 × #11)		
13.	Credit for Returned Merchandise (#4 × #2a)		
14.	Net Profit per Order (#12 + #13)		
15.	Cost per Thousand Contacts (Marketing Expense)		
16.	Number of Orders per Thousand Needed to Break Even (#15 ÷ #14)		

About the Authors

John Stockwell is President of Diadem, Inc., a full-service direct response advertising agency in Englewood Cliffs, New Jersey. He is also the founder of National Card Pack Center, a card pack management and sales firm in the same city. He has extensive experience in direct marketing, having held positions of copywriter, copy chief, and manager of direct mail operations with McGraw-Hill and other companies. His clients include those in business, professional, medical, and high-tech fields. In addition, he has given lectures and seminars on direct response topics in the United States and abroad and is the author of more than a dozen business books.

Henry M. Shaw is President of Merceret Associates, Inc., a marketing consulting firm in Old Tappan, New Jersey. He holds an M.A. from the University of Colorado and an M.B.A. from Fordham University. His consulting assignments have ranged from direct mail planning to marketing research to strategic analysis for publishers, consulting firms, trade associations, and retailers. He has been copywriter, salesperson, product manager, national exhibits manager, direct mail manager, marketing services director, and marketing director at the McGraw-Hill Book Company. He also teaches marketing and advertising and promotion in the evening at a local college.